Guideposts
Daily Planner
2026

Forgetting what is behind and straining toward what is ahead...
—PHILIPPIANS 3:13 (NIV)

LIVING A NEW LIFE
Releasing the Old Year

My children and grandchildren left to celebrate the new year with their friends. The lovely silence of the house nestles around me as I settle into my prayer chair for a ritual I've practiced for several years. I turn off the lamp on the end table, light a candle, and remember the year, month by month.

I still feel strong emotions as I recall those things that marred the year—arguments, tears and losses, hurricanes, wars of greed, and a relationship that ended. It's hard to let the pain go. But there are also happy memories I want to cling to: the moment of my granddaughter's birth; a favored friendship; a fresh spiritual insight; a satisfying work project; a trip to California.

Life is change. I need to remind myself that endings lead to beginnings, and that even good things must be held lightly in order to grow. So one by one I offer them up, the sad ones and the glad ones, knowing that forever and in all ways these released events of the past year are safe with God.

Now, as the clock nears midnight, I sit quietly in the stillness, feeling lighter and freer. The future, still a mystery, glistens with the promise of a Light beyond time, a Light that shines in the darkness, a Light that cradles overflowing hope.

—*Marilyn Morgan Helleberg*

A PRAYER FOR JANUARY

For the new year
The new beginning
The growing light
The coming spring
Your ever-present love
We praise you, Lord
With our lips
Our hearts
And our steps

UNKNOWN

JANUARY 2026

SUNDAY	MONDAY	TUESDAY	WEDNESDAY	THURSDAY	FRIDAY	SATURDAY
				1 NEW YEAR'S DAY	2	3
4	5	6 EPIPHANY	7	8	9	10
11	12	13	14	15	16	17
18	19 MARTIN LUTHER KING JR. DAY	20	21	22	23	24
25	26	27	28	29	30	31

NOTES

DECEMBER 2025

S	M	T	W	T	F	S
	1	2	3	4	5	6
7	8	9	10	11	12	13
14	15	16	17	18	19	20
21	22	23	24	25	26	27
28	29	30	31			

FEBRUARY

S	M	T	W	T	F	S
1	2	3	4	5	6	7
8	9	10	11	12	13	14
15	16	17	18	19	20	21
22	23	24	25	26	27	28

GUIDEPOSTS DAILY PLANNER

OUR PRAYER

Father, help us to remember that even as we put away our treasures of the past, You have even greater treasures of the future waiting for us.

DEC 2025

28 SUNDAY

Share with the Lord's people who are in need. Practice hospitality. —Romans 12:13 (NIV)

---

29 MONDAY

Let the heavens rejoice, let the earth be glad; let the sea resound, and all that is in it. Let the fields be jubilant, and everything in them; let all the trees of the forest sing for joy. —Psalm 96:11–12 (NIV)

---

30 TUESDAY

Speak the truth to each other.... —Zechariah 8:16 (NIV)

"I don't want Christmas to be over yet," our 10-year-old said as we prepared for our New Year's celebrations. "How soon do we have to take down the tree?"

"As soon as possible, Mark. It's shedding." I rumpled his hair and kissed him. "We can't hang on to everything we want to, honey. Life keeps changing."

To my surprise, he shrugged, then sprang from my arms and grabbed a handful of tinsel. "OK," he yelled at those trailing in, "let's have a race to see who can take the most stuff off the tree before midnight when the whistles blow!"

"And put it away!" I interrupted, rushing for sacks and boxes, and laughing at the merry commotion. But like my son, I was already a little homesick for the year we were about to tell goodbye. I wanted to hang on to it a little longer—the fun and adventures we'd shared, and even the pain and problems. I longed to see if I couldn't do better: have more faith; be more patient and wiser. I didn't want the new year; I just wanted another chance at the old one!

But now, tonight, I'm caught up in the excitement again. The bells are clanging, whistles blowing, fireworks lighting the sky. "Don't look back," everything

31
WEDNESDAY
NEW YEAR'S EVE

And the Lord . . . will be with thee, he will not fail thee, neither forsake thee: fear not, neither be dismayed. —Deuteronomy 31:8 (KJV)

JANUARY 1
THURSDAY
NEW YEAR'S DAY

God said, Let there be light: and there was light. —Genesis 1:3 (KJV)

2
FRIDAY

He shall direct thy paths. —Proverbs 3:6 (KJV)

3
SATURDAY

He is your example, and you must follow in his steps. —1 Peter 2:21 (NLT)

---

seems to be calling. "Look ahead!" And they are right. How wonderful that every year God hands us this shining new package of time, filled with hope and promise, which can be revealed only when we have stripped off the final wrappings of the old.

—*Marjorie Holmes*

PRAYER REQUESTS _____

_____

_____

JANUARY

S	M	T	W	T	F	S
				1	2	3
4	5	6	7	8	9	10
11	12	13	14	15	16	17
18	19	20	21	22	23	24
25	26	27	28	29	30	31

GUIDEPOSTS DAILY PLANNER

OUR PRAYER

Lord, may Your blessing be on all our houses, so that our homes may radiate Your love and peace.

4 SUNDAY

Write them on the tablet of your heart. —Proverbs 7:3 (NIV)

5 MONDAY

Welcome one another, therefore, just as Christ has welcomed you, for the glory of God. —Romans 15:7 (NRSVUE)

6 TUESDAY
EPIPHANY

We have seen his star in the East, and have come to worship him. —Matthew 2:2 (RSV)

FOR 5 YEARS I rented the third floor of my house to a young couple with a growing family—and growing problems. I enjoyed the babies, and often babysat. But over the years the parents' arguments and fights increased in number and intensity. Then the husband moved out, leaving his wife with three small children.

Eventually they, too, moved out, and I spent June through August having the apartment refurbished and trying to find a tenant.

After a few months, another young couple with a baby moved in. But they, too, fought and argued. In two months, they had broken up and moved out.

"The walls of the apartment must be soaked with ugly words, angry cries, tears, and the sounds of violence," I said to my friend Tessie at church. "How do I counteract that?"

"Why not have a house blessing service?" she said.

That was my answer. Some time before Christmas, Pastor Clemente came over and we prayed through the apartment, asking God to remove any negative influence and make it a place of serenity.

The next person who came to see the apartment was a young professional woman. That very evening we agreed on the details, and she moved in at the

7
WEDNESDAY

Every morning he makes me eager to hear what he is going to teach me.
—Isaiah 50:4 (GNT)

8
THURSDAY

For we walk by faith, not by sight. —2 Corinthians 5:7 (NKJV)

9
FRIDAY

Yet to all who received him, to those who believed in his name, he gave the right to become children of God. —John 1:12 (NIV)

10
SATURDAY

Against all hope, Abraham in hope believed. —Romans 4:18 (NIV)

JANUARY

beginning of January. She's quiet and considerate—and, I discovered afterward, a practicing Christian. "This apartment has been a real blessing," she said to me recently.

"A blessing—and blessed," I replied, and then I told her why.

—*Mary Ruth Howes*

PRAYER REQUESTS _____

_____

_____

_____

JANUARY

S	M	T	W	T	F	S
				1	2	3
4	5	6	7	8	9	10
11	12	13	14	15	16	17
18	19	20	21	22	23	24
25	26	27	28	29	30	31

GUIDEPOSTS DAILY PLANNER

OUR PRAYER
Lord Jesus, thank You for showing us the face of the Father. Help us, through faith, to accept His love.

---

11 SUNDAY

The God of all comfort . . . comforts us in all our troubles, so that we can comfort those in any trouble with the comfort we ourselves receive from God. —2 Corinthians 1:3–4 (NIV)

---

12 MONDAY

We will tell the next generation the praiseworthy deeds of the Lord. —Psalm 78:4 (NIV)

---

13 TUESDAY

Though your sins are like scarlet, they shall be as white as snow. —Isaiah 1:18 (ESV)

I was astonished to tears at the lifelike oil portrait my artist friend Eva Llanos did for the three- to five-year-olds' Sunday school classroom. It was a copy of the famous one by Frances Hook, where Jesus is holding a child's face in both of His strong, carpenter's hands. The outstanding feature of this picture is the unconditional love burning in Jesus's eyes as He gazes into the face of this child.

I hung it over our altar where we gather for storytime and worship. But it wasn't just the children who were mesmerized. The adults, too, came to see. Early one Sunday, a woman I didn't know came in and stood for a long time not saying anything, just looking over the altar into the picture. Finally, I heard her whisper, "I wish my father would have looked at me like that."

14 WEDNESDAY

Where can I go from your Spirit? Where can I flee from your presence?
—Psalm 139:7 (NIV)

15 THURSDAY

What does the LORD require of you? To act justly and to love mercy and to walk humbly with your God. —Micah 6:8 (NIV)

16 FRIDAY

"Ask, and it will be given you; search, and you will find; knock, and the door will be opened for you." —Luke 11:9 (NRSVCE)

17 SATURDAY

We need not fear even if the world blows up and the mountains crumble into the sea.
—Psalm 46:2 (TLB)

JANUARY

I didn't answer. She wasn't talking to me. But a moment later her face lit up like the child's in the picture, and I knew God had slipped the truth into her heart: Her Father does look at her like that. And at you and me.

—*Shari Smyth*

PRAYER REQUESTS _____

JANUARY

S	M	T	W	T	F	S
					1	2	3
4	5	6	7	8	9	10
11	12	13	14	15	16	17
18	19	20	21	22	23	24
25	26	27	28	29	30	31

GUIDEPOSTS DAILY PLANNER

OUR PRAYER
Lord, thank You for making my burdens light with Your love.

---

18 SUNDAY
You have given me the heritage of those who fear your name. —Psalm 61:5 (NRSVUE)

---

19 MONDAY
MARTIN LUTHER KING JR. DAY

Remember the days of old; consider the years of many generations; ask your father, and he will show you, your elders, and they will tell you. —Deuteronomy 32:7 (ESV)

---

20 TUESDAY
Knowledge puffs up while love builds up. —1 Corinthians 8:1 (NIV)

I FELT A LOT like a cartoon character with an ever-present rain cloud looming over my head. Tomorrow's forecast had major storm fronts gathering for me, chemistry test third period, trigonometry for fifth and an oral report on John Steinbeck's *The Grapes of Wrath* scheduled for eighth. I began to think of the Joad family's travails as a vacation lark compared to what I had to face on Friday.

My bedroom floor was awash with texts and scattered notes, and I looked around frantically for some kind of organizational life raft to cling to. My annoyance sonar was finely tuned to the slightest distractions and, naturally, distractions were everywhere. I heard a car's door slam and flew to the window to glower.

Instead, I saw my childhood pal Paulie, now 17, and his mom arriving home. I had forgotten that Thursday was my old friend's chemotherapy day, and I watched as Paul, slighter and seemingly more vulnerable now than he had been at 10, shuffled his way tiredly up his front steps. Pausing to catch his breath, he noticed me, smiled wanly, and called with effort, "Nice day, huh, Jen? How's it goin'?"

JANUARY 2026

21 WEDNESDAY

Jesus answered, "Everyone who drinks this water will be thirsty again, but whoever drinks the water I give them will never thirst." —John 4:13–14 (NIV)

22 THURSDAY

[The lepers] called out in a loud voice, "Jesus, Master, have pity on us!" When he saw them, he said, "Go, show yourselves to the priests." And as they went, they were cleansed. —Luke 17:13–14 (NIV)

23 FRIDAY

Abraham called that place The Lord Will Provide. And to this day it is said, "On the mountain of the Lord it will be provided." —Genesis 22:14 (NIV)

24 SATURDAY

Sing to the Lord a new song, for he has done marvelous things. —Psalm 98:1 (NIV)

At that moment, with a sure and direct hand, God cleared the clouds above me and gave me pause to see with a clearer perspective. I shot Paulie a "thumbs up" and managed to choke out, "Got it made, Paulie! I got it made!"

—Jenny Mutzbauer

PRAYER REQUESTS _____

JANUARY

S	M	T	W	T	F	S
					1	2	3
4	5	6	7	8	9	10
11	12	13	14	15	16	17
18	19	20	21	22	23	24
25	26	27	28	29	30	31

GUIDEPOSTS DAILY PLANNER

OUR PRAYER
Father, help me to see the lighter side of things.

25 SUNDAY
"Come," [Jesus] said. Then Peter got down out of the boat, walked on the water and came toward Jesus. —Matthew 14:29 (NIV)

26 MONDAY
Children are a heritage from the LORD, offspring a reward from him. Like arrows in the hands of a warrior are children born in one's youth. —Psalm 127:3–4 (NIV)

27 TUESDAY
While we have opportunity, let's do good to all people. —Galatians 6:10 (NASB)

I WAS BABYSITTING three of my grandchildren, and it was time to bathe 2-year-old Thomas. I got him and all his toys into the tub and began to wash him, sitting at an angle on the edge so I could continue talking with Jamie and Katie, his sisters. Then, before I could catch myself, I lost my balance, slipped backward and fell into the tub—fully clothed!

My granddaughters laughed hysterically. Thomas, observing them for a few seconds, threw his head back and joined in the laughter. As I sat in the warm water with my arms and legs extended, I felt this tremendous laugh making its way out. I leaned against the pink tiles and let it come. The four of us were joined together by our laughter, which lasted for perhaps 3 minutes and was exhausting and satisfying and unforgettable.

Of course, I wouldn't have laughed in my young motherhood days. I would have resented anything that made me look less than perfect and would have been in a nasty mood for the rest of the evening,

28
WEDNESDAY

May the Lord direct your hearts to the love of God and to the perseverance of Christ. —2 Thessalonians 3:5 (NASB)

29
THURSDAY

A joyful heart is good medicine. —Proverbs 17:22 (ESV)

30
FRIDAY

Post this at all the intersections, dear friends: Lead with your ears, follow up with your tongue, and let anger straggle along in the rear. —James 1:19 (MSG)

31
SATURDAY

Be joyful in hope, patient in affliction, faithful in prayer. —Romans 12:12 (NIV)

JANUARY

probably not speaking. And we would never have mentioned the incident again.

I'm glad I have finally learned—through experience, age, and God's grace—that there's a time to laugh, even at myself and my humanness.

—*Marion Bond West*

PRAYER REQUESTS

JANUARY

S	M	T	W	T	F	S
				1	2	3
4	5	6	7	8	9	10
11	12	13	14	15	16	17
18	19	20	21	22	23	24
25	26	27	28	29	30	31

GUIDEPOSTS DAILY PLANNER

But he who endures to the end shall be saved. —MARK 13:13 (NKJV)

A PRAYER FOR FEBRUARY

O Father God,
Silent are Your woods now
Where the snows lie deep.
The days are rimed with frost,
The nights are long.
The world's asleep, dreaming of sunshine,
Waiting for spring to come
With its warm green kiss
That wakens everything. . . .
Speak to my waiting soul, Lord,
Call me into the warmth of Your presence,
And Your love.

DAILY GUIDEPOSTS 1980

LIVING A NEW LIFE
Lay the First Brick

The other day I found myself in the First African Baptist Church in my hometown, Savannah, Georgia. It stands facing Franklin Square, gaunt and angular, with a certain power that is hard to explain unless you know something about its history.

It was built by slaves just at the beginning of the Civil War. Their owners allowed them to work on it at night by the light of bonfires after their other tasks were done. Records of the construction are almost nonexistent, except for a single phrase in an old ledger: "The man who laid the first brick was the man who laid the last."

Who was that man? I imagine it must have been the person who led the effort, one of their own number, a person who laid the first brick with faith and hope and determination, and then four years later laid the last. No one knows for certain who that leader was, but the church is his monument and his glory.

More often than I like to acknowledge, I have become discouraged in the middle of a project. Sometimes I have given up altogether. But now I think I have a phrase to remember when that temptation comes, when the going gets tough, when it's much easier for me to stop than go on. *The man who laid the first brick laid the last.*

—Arthur Gordon

FEBRUARY 2026

SUNDAY	MONDAY	TUESDAY	WEDNESDAY	THURSDAY	FRIDAY	SATURDAY
1	2	3	4	5	6	7
8	9	10	11	12 ABRAHAM LINCOLN'S BIRTHDAY	13	14 VALENTINE'S DAY
15	16 PRESIDENT'S DAY	17	18 ASH WEDNESDAY	19	20	21
22 GEORGE WASHINGTON'S BIRTHDAY	23	24	25	26	27	28

NOTES

JANUARY

S	M	T	W	T	F	S
				1	2	3
4	5	6	7	8	9	10
11	12	13	14	15	16	17
18	19	20	21	22	23	24
25	26	27	28	29	30	31

MARCH

S	M	T	W	T	F	S
1	2	3	4	5	6	7
8	9	10	11	12	13	14
15	16	17	18	19	20	21
22	23	24	25	26	27	28
29	30	31				

GUIDEPOSTS DAILY PLANNER

OUR PRAYER
Today, Lord, remind me that Your plan for me is always, without a doubt, the best plan—no matter what.

1 SUNDAY — If I then, your Lord and Teacher, have washed your feet, you also ought to wash one another's feet. —John 13:14 (ESV)

2 MONDAY — A friend loves at all times, and a brother is born for a time of adversity. —Proverbs 17:17 (NIV)

3 TUESDAY — The Lord is good to all; he has compassion on all he has made. —Psalm 145:9 (NIV)

For many years, when the University of Wisconsin Badgers football team wasn't doing so well, we still had our spectacular marching band. Everybody loved their wild and crazy "fifth quarter" presentation after each game. But one fall, something wonderful happened. The Badgers had a 10-1-1 season and made it to the Rose Bowl for the first time in 31 years!

Armed with his recent "Most Valuable Percussionist" award, my son Michael and his fellow Badger band members were off to Pasadena. Oh, how I wanted to go to that game! I searched my savings and checking accounts, desperately trying to figure out a way to afford the airfare and hotel costs. I entered a newspaper contest where the prize was a trip to the game. I warned my out-of-state relatives who were planning to come to my home for New Year's weekend that I might be going to the game in person.

Well, none of it happened. I stayed home, the relatives came (all thirteen of them!), and we watched Michael on TV as the camera focused in on him playing his duos and high-stepping his way through the most exciting day of his life. And

4
WEDNESDAY

Miriam the prophet, Aaron's sister, took a timbrel in her hand, and all the women followed her, with timbrels and dancing. —Exodus 15:20 (NIV)

5
THURSDAY

He will wipe every tear from their eyes. There will be no more death or mourning or crying or pain, for the old order of things has passed away. —Revelation 21:4 (NIV)

6
FRIDAY

He has made everything beautiful in its time. —Ecclesiastes 3:11 (NIV)

7
SATURDAY

Above all, love each other deeply, because love covers over a multitude of sins. —1 Peter 4:8 (NIV)

---

we cheered, laughed, whooped, and hollered as we watched our team win in an upset.

We humans don't always know what's best for us, but God sure does. I was much better off with my big family in my own home than I would have been in Pasadena—and I got to see my son clearly on his proudest day.

—*Patricia Lorenz*

PRAYER REQUESTS _____

FEBRUARY

S	M	T	W	T	F	S
1	2	3	4	5	6	7
8	9	10	11	12	13	14
15	16	17	18	19	20	21
22	23	24	25	26	27	28

OUR PRAYER
Lord, teach me how to open my times of waiting to Your grace.

---

8 SUNDAY

Let us consider one another in order to stir up love and good works. —Hebrews 10:24 (NKJV)

---

9 MONDAY

For we know that if the earthly tent we live in is destroyed, we have a building from God, an eternal house in heaven, not built by human hands. —2 Corinthians 5:1 (NIV)

---

10 TUESDAY

[King David's] servants covered him with blankets. —1 Kings 1:1 (GNT)

I WAS STANDING in line at the grocery store, waiting to check out. The woman at the head of the line had even more than I, and since she kept chatting with the clerk, it was taking a long time. Most of us in the line were shifting grumpily from one foot to the other.

The line grew, snaking through the displays. I sighed impatiently, catching the eye of an elderly man who was standing just behind me. He returned my wry smile with a warm smile of his own. *What a nice man.* A bit of my annoyance drained away.

I noticed that he had only one item, a small bag of mushrooms. As the woman at the head of the line began moving her cart at last, I nodded at him. "You've only got one thing, and I have so many. Why don't you just go ahead of me?"

"No," he said, smiling his lovely smile again, "thanks just the same. You know, I've made a study and I've discovered that I have to spend 16 percent of my life waiting. So I decided that I should learn how to wait graciously."

I've never forgotten that man. I have no idea how he came up with his 16 percent figure, but

FEBRUARY 2026

11 WEDNESDAY

Do not conform to the pattern of this world, but be transformed by the renewing of your mind. Then you will be able to test and approve what God's will is—his good, pleasing and perfect will. —Romans 12:2 (NIV)

12 THURSDAY
ABRAHAM LINCOLN'S BIRTHDAY

Do you not know that your bodies are temples of the Holy Spirit, who is in you, whom you have received from God? You are not your own. —1 Corinthians 6:19 (NIV)

13 FRIDAY

For whoever has despised the day of small things shall rejoice. —Zechariah 4:10 (RSV)

14 SATURDAY
VALENTINE'S DAY

Tell the Israelite people to bring Me gifts. —Exodus 25:2 (JPS)

FEBRUARY

15 years later he still comes to mind when I am forced to wait by people or circumstances. I am still trying to learn to wait graciously, to slow myself down—to think, as he did, of the other people in a tiresome line.

—*Katherine Paterson*

PRAYER REQUESTS _____

FEBRUARY

S	M	T	W	T	F	S
1	2	3	4	5	6	7
8	9	10	11	12	13	14
15	16	17	18	19	20	21
22	23	24	25	26	27	28

GUIDEPOSTS DAILY PLANNER

OUR PRAYER

As we remember Your pain and the suffering of Your passion, beloved Lord Jesus, we ask for Your forgiveness and healing grace.

---

15 SUNDAY

The Lord will rescue me from every evil attack and will bring me safely to his heavenly kingdom. —2 Timothy 4:18 (NIV)

---

16 MONDAY
PRESIDENTS' DAY

Show proper respect to everyone, love the family of believers, fear God, honor the emperor. —1 Peter 2:17 (NIV)

---

17 TUESDAY

Now is the acceptable time; look, now is the day of salvation! —2 Corinthians 6:2 (NRSVUE)

IN CHURCH LAST SUNDAY, we were given small slips of paper at our morning services. "Write on them," we were told, "those things in your lives that you would like to put under the mercy of the Lord. Pain from a memory or a current hurt. Sins confessed. The need to forgive someone who has offended you. A habit that needs breaking. The commitment to help a homeless family."

All over the congregation there were tears as we wrote. Then we came to the front of the church and one by one we placed these small pieces of our lives onto smoldering coals in an urn, to be burnt and turned into ash. These are the ashes that today, Ash Wednesday—the beginning of Lent—will be used to mark our foreheads with the sign of the cross—a reminder of our own mortality and the sacrificial death of our Lord and Savior, Jesus Christ.

As my forehead is marked, I think of those intermingled ashes—my pain, with other people's

FEBRUARY 2026

18
WEDNESDAY
ASH WEDNESDAY

For as the heaven is high above the earth, so great is his mercy toward them that fear him. As far as the east is from the west, so far hath he removed our transgressions from us. —Psalm 103:11–12 (KJV)

19
THURSDAY

In his kindness God called you to share in his eternal glory by means of Christ Jesus. —1 Peter 5:10 (NLT)

20
FRIDAY

We rejoice in our sufferings, knowing that suffering produces endurance, and endurance produces character, and character produces hope. —Romans 5:3–4 (ESV)

21
SATURDAY

Many waters cannot quench love, nor can rivers drown it. If a man tried to buy love with all his wealth, his offer would be utterly scorned. —Song of Solomon 8:7 (NLT)

---

pain, mixed together and given to the Lord. They not only speak to me of our common humanity, but they also point to the ultimate answer to suffering: Christ's forgiveness, His healing and His resurrection power!

—Fay Angus

PRAYER REQUESTS _____

FEBRUARY

S	M	T	W	T	F	S
1	2	3	4	5	6	7
8	9	10	11	12	13	14
15	16	17	18	19	20	21
22	23	24	25	26	27	28

GUIDEPOSTS DAILY PLANNER

OUR PRAYER

Today, Lord, help me to humbly serve others, creating precedents that will last for generations.

---

22 SUNDAY
GEORGE WASHINGTON'S BIRTHDAY

Those who cling to worthless idols turn away from God's love for them. —Jonah 2:8 (NIV)

---

23 MONDAY

I was sick, and you visited Me. —Matthew 25:36 (NKJV)

---

24 TUESDAY

Now to the King eternal, immortal, invisible, the only God, be honor and glory for ever and ever. Amen. —1 Timothy 1:17 (NIV)

During a three-day visit to Philadelphia, I toured Congress Hall, Independence Hall, and Carpenter's Hall—restored buildings that tell the secrets of where and how the Declaration of Independence was written and where the first presidency was carried out.

I felt a sense of awe as I gazed at the elaborate silver inkstand used to sign the Declaration of Independence more than 200 years ago, and then ran my hand down the banister on the same stairway George Washington used in Independence Hall during his two terms as president from 1789 to 1797.

What amazed me most about my trip through American history was Washington's humility. Our guide told us that Washington refused to serve more than two terms as president, even though he would have been easily reelected to a third term. Rather than follow the example of England's monarchs who ruled for their lifetime, Washington felt that no U.S. president should be in power more than 8 years.

Today, on George Washington's birthday, what act of humility can we practice that could set a precedent for our families? Perhaps planning a vacation centered on the interests of other members

25
WEDNESDAY

Your basket and your kneading trough will be blessed. —Deuteronomy 28:5 (NIV)

26
THURSDAY

May the Lord give you discretion and understanding. —1 Chronicles 22:12 (NIV)

27
FRIDAY

I will remember the deeds of the Lord; yes, I will remember your miracles of long ago. —Psalm 77:11 (NIV)

28
SATURDAY

From him the whole body, joined and held together by every supporting ligament, grows and builds itself up in love, as each part does its work. —Ephesians 4:16 (NIV)

---

of the family instead of our own. Or quietly doing things for them without any announcement. If we humble ourselves by being servants to those we love, perhaps we'll be revered in God's eyes the way Washington was revered by his countrymen.

—*Patricia Lorenz*

PRAYER REQUESTS _____

FEBRUARY

S	M	T	W	T	F	S
1	2	3	4	5	6	7
8	9	10	11	12	13	14
15	16	17	18	19	20	21
22	23	24	25	26	27	28

GUIDEPOSTS DAILY PLANNER

O Lord, you have searched me and known me. —PSALM 139:1 (NRSVUE)

LIVING A NEW LIFE
A Lovestruck Mother

On the June morning 30 years ago when my son was first put into my arms, I waited until the nurse was out of the room and then, my eye still on the door, I pulled loose the deftly bound blanket and began to examine the tiny person it had hidden.

He seemed perfect to me, even the crooked little toes, so like his father's large ones. I marveled, as any new mother might, that this wonderful child had grown for these past nine months inside my body.

And I wasn't the only one. Everyone thought he was beautiful. The first words the nurse had said in the delivery room were, "Look at those eyelashes! Wouldn't you know? Wasted on a boy."

Someday, I thought, stroking his silky cheek, *someday, he's going to have to shave.* I laughed aloud at the thought.

As I held my son each morning, I saw the Parent of us all bending in love over me. The marvel we share in God's creation is nothing new, yet it is new for every parent at every birth. It reminds me that God not only made me, God loves me, searching me with the eyes of a lovestruck mother marveling over her newborn child.

—*Katherine Paterson*

A PRAYER FOR MARCH

Today, Lord, let my life be a prayer,
Let me be so close to You
that You become a part of my every conversation.
Let me be open to Your presence
so that I sense Your power at work in the world You created.
Let me be so filled with your love,
it flows out to others.
Today, Lord, today— let my life
   be a prayer.

UNKNOWN

MARCH 2026

SUNDAY	MONDAY	TUESDAY	WEDNESDAY	THURSDAY	FRIDAY	SATURDAY
1	2	3	4	5	6	7
8 DAYLIGHT SAVING TIME BEGINS	9	10	11	12	13	14
15	16	17 ST. PATRICK'S DAY	18	19	20 SPRING BEGINS	21
22	23	24	25	26	27	28
29 PALM SUNDAY	30	31				

NOTES

FEBRUARY

S	M	T	W	T	F	S
1	2	3	4	5	6	7
8	9	10	11	12	13	14
15	16	17	18	19	20	21
22	23	24	25	26	27	28

APRIL

S	M	T	W	T	F	S
			1	2	3	4
5	6	7	8	9	10	11
12	13	14	15	16	17	18
19	20	21	22	23	24	25
26	27	28	29	30		

GUIDEPOSTS DAILY PLANNER

OUR PRAYER
Heavenly Father, thank you for the power of Your love to lift us up and give us fortitude and hope.

1 SUNDAY
Be firm and be calm. —Isaiah 7:4 (JPS)

2 MONDAY
They sought God eagerly, and he was found by them. —2 Chronicles 15:15 (NIV)

3 TUESDAY
"I have the right to do anything"—but I will not be mastered by anything. —1 Corinthians 6:12 (NIV)

When my friend Paula learned that she had breast cancer, she became fearful and depressed. She and I called around town looking for a healing service and found that St. John's Episcopal Cathedral here in Albuquerque, New Mexico, holds one every Tuesday morning at 10 o'clock. We went together to the service. When the priest spoke of the power of faith and prayer, the presence of Jesus filled the room with an almost tangible force.

Then Paula went up to the altar rail, where the priest prayed for her and anointed her head with oil. As he did so, she told me later, she felt strength surge through her body, along with renewed hope for eventual recovery.

Although she did have to have a mastectomy, followed by chemotherapy, Paula said that the continued prayers of that church and of loved ones sustained her throughout her treatment. "I could feel those prayers. I could feel the energy," she says. "They gave me the strength and courage to face some really bad days."

Because of my friend's experience, I've learned

4
WEDNESDAY

Let us run with endurance the race God has set before us. —Hebrews 12:1 (NLT)

5
THURSDAY

Jesus Christ is the same yesterday and today and forever. —Hebrews 13:8 (NIV)

6
FRIDAY

Wake up! Strengthen what remains and is about to die, for I have found your deeds unfinished in the sight of my God. —Revelation 3:2 (NIV)

7
SATURDAY

Your eyes saw my unformed body; all the days ordained for me were written in your book before one of them came to be. —Psalm 139:16 (NIV)

---

to keep on praying, for others and also for myself, even when the body falters and the way looks dark. For the strengthening of the spirit that comes from Christ—that is the true "healing" that can see us through.

—*Madge Harrah*

PRAYER REQUESTS _____

MARCH

S	M	T	W	T	F	S
	1	2	3	4	5	6	7
8	9	10	11	12	13	14
15	16	17	18	19	20	21
22	23	24	25	26	27	28
29	30	31				

OUR PRAYER

Lord, please guide our young people through adolescence into adulthood with Your great love and care.

8
SUNDAY
DAYLIGHT SAVING TIME BEGINS

This vision is for a future time. It describes the end, and it will be fulfilled. If it seems slow in coming, wait patiently, for it will surely take place. It will not be delayed. —Habakkuk 2:3 (NLT)

9
MONDAY

But He said to them, "Beware, and be on your guard against every form of greed." —Luke 12:15 (NASB)

10
TUESDAY

Look carefully then how you walk, not as unwise but as wise. —Ephesians 5:15 (ESV)

When my son Michael was 11, he bought for me a large picture of Christ with a light attached just below it. I loved the picture, and we used it for a night-light.

When he was about 16, some problems started, the kind that many teenagers have. Michael became rebellious and defiant, and refused to come in at his curfew. I could never go to bed while he was out, and one night he stepped belligerently into the living room to find me up—again. He looked straight at the picture of Christ. "Why do you always leave this light on for me?" he demanded.

"We've been leaving it on for about 5 years now for anyone who is out," I responded.

"Well, don't leave it on anymore," he said. "I don't like to walk in here at night and see Him staring at me like that, first thing." I smelled beer on his breath and recoiled in shock.

His father had a long and serious talk with him the next day about his attitude and his actions. I did not wait up for Michael that night, nor did I leave the light on, not for the rest of the week. But I heard him coming in, and he was coming in on time every night now.

MARCH 2026

11 WEDNESDAY

See! The winter is past; the rains are over and gone. Flowers appear on the earth; the season of singing has come, the cooing of doves is heard in our land. —Song of Songs 2:11–12 (NIV)

12 THURSDAY

For now we see only a reflection, as in a mirror, but then we will see face to face. Now I know only in part; then I will know fully, even as I have been fully known. —1 Corinthians 13:12 (NRSVUE)

13 FRIDAY

I meditate on your precepts and consider your ways. —Psalm 119:15 (NIV)

14 SATURDAY

May he give you the desire of your heart and make all your plans succeed. —Psalm 20:4 (NIV)

Then one evening he said, "I'm just going to the movie, Mama, but leave the light on for me, will you?" At the door, he turned and looked back at me. His eyes met mine with full force. "I've kinda missed Him lighting my way in."

—Dorothy Nicholas

PRAYER REQUESTS ____________________

____

____

____

MARCH

S	M	T	W	T	F	S
1	2	3	4	5	6	7
8	9	10	11	12	13	14
15	16	17	18	19	20	21
22	23	24	25	26	27	28
29	30	31				

OUR PRAYER

Dear Lord, give me the grace to remember that You are ready to embrace me, if I am willing to take one step toward You.

---

15 SUNDAY

For I the LORD do not change. —Malachi 3:6 (RSV)

---

16 MONDAY

Being confident of this, that he who began a good work in you will carry it on to completion until the day of Christ Jesus. —Philippians 1:6 (NIV)

---

17 TUESDAY
ST. PATRICK'S DAY

Wait for the LORD; be strong and take heart and wait for the LORD. —Psalm 27:14 (NIV)

"A LONELY MAN and a distant God. A lonely man and a distant God. A lonely man . . ." The rhythmic pounding of my feet matched the repetition of my words, words that matched my mood—heavy.

On this cold March evening, I had felt the need for a run. Winter had been hard and dreary. I had been grinding out unsatisfying work. My family and I were all busy about our own tasks and had little to do with one another. Although I was sure all of us loved one another, this winter I experienced little emotional warmth.

Somewhere around the third mile, I realized that my tongue had turned the incantation around without my being aware of it. Now I was repeating, "A lonely God and a distant man. A lonely God and a distant man. . . ."

It was true. I was lonely. But it wasn't God who had been distant. I had pulled myself away from Him—and from my family.

A lonely God and a distant man? No more. I stopped myself in mid-run and turned toward home.

"I have always known that when you are miserable you withdraw from people, but now I know you

MARCH 2026

18
WEDNESDAY

Only be careful, and watch yourselves closely so that you do not forget the things your eyes have seen or let them fade from your heart as long as you live. —Deuteronomy 4:9 (NIV)

19
THURSDAY

For the eyes of the Lord run to and fro. —2 Chronicles 16:9 (KJV)

20
FRIDAY

SPRING BEGINS

Fear not, for I am with you; be not dismayed, for I am your God; I will strengthen you, I will help you, I will uphold you with my righteous right hand. —Isaiah 41:10 (ESV)

21
SATURDAY

This is my command—be strong and courageous! Do not be afraid or discouraged. For the Lord your God is with you wherever you go. —Joshua 1:9 (NLT)

---

withdraw from God, too," my wife commented after I told her about my run. "If you decide to move toward Him, will you put me next on the list?"

"Do you think we still have time to light a fire in the fireplace?" I replied.

—*John Cowan*

PRAYER REQUESTS _____

_____

_____

MARCH

S	M	T	W	T	F	S
						1
1	2	3	4	5	6	7
8	9	10	11	12	13	14
15	16	17	18	19	20	21
22	23	24	25	26	27	28
29	30	31				

OUR PRAYER

Father, help me not only to remember the past with fondness, but to live joyfully in the present.

---

22 SUNDAY

My sheep listen to my voice; I know them, and they follow me. I give them eternal life, and they shall never perish; no one will snatch them out of my hand. —John 10:27–28 (NIV)

---

23 MONDAY

I have my eye on salt-of-the-earth people—they're the ones I want working with me; . . . But no one who traffics in lies gets a job with me; I have no patience with liars. —Psalm 101:6, 8 (MSG)

---

24 TUESDAY

The pleasantness of a friend springs from their heartfelt advice. —Proverbs 27:9 (NIV)

Not long after I turned 70, I got a letter from my longtime friend Flo. Opening it, I found a yellowed envelope addressed, in my handwriting, *For Isabel. Open when you're 70.* Inside, I read what Flo and I, in our mid-twenties back then, had wanted to be reminded of 50 years later.

"Senior citizens are such bores!" We were complaining about the exasperating habits of several elderly folk we knew.

"Do not talk about your health. Do not repeat the same old stories."

Flo and I had laughed as we dashed off the items.

"Do not offer advice. Do not criticize the choir, pastor, church members, younger people . . .

"Do not refer to your Good Old Days!"

I had put the sheet of paper in an envelope, addressed it and given it to Flo. "Keep this for me," I told her, "and return it to me when I turn 70." And we laughed again, never expecting to live that long.

Now, with the list in my hand, I was hearing myself tell my sons that their children could stand a little more discipline. And that "we used to worship

MARCH 2026

25
WEDNESDAY

We know that in all things God works for the good of those who love him, who have been called according to his purpose. —Romans 8:28 (NIV)

26
THURSDAY

Therefore encourage one another and build each other up, just as in fact you are doing. —1 Thessalonians 5:11 (NIV)

27
FRIDAY

Therefore we do not lose heart. Though outwardly we are wasting away, yet inwardly we are being renewed day by day. —2 Corinthians 4:16 (NIV)

28
SATURDAY

This is love: not that we loved God, but that he loved us and sent his Son as an atoning sacrifice for our sins. —1 John 4:10 (NIV)

MARCH

as a family, remember?" when the grandchildren sat with their peers in church. And how many times had I boasted how good things were in the old days after reading about all the evils of the present day? I laughed ruefully, caught by my own words.

—*Isabel Wolseley*

PRAYER REQUESTS _____

MARCH

S	M	T	W	T	F	S
1	2	3	4	5	6	7
8	9	10	11	12	13	14
15	16	17	18	19	20	21
22	23	24	25	26	27	28
29	30	31				

GUIDEPOSTS DAILY PLANNER

There are diversities of gifts, but the same Spirit. —1 CORINTHIANS 12:4 (NKJV)

A PRAYER FOR APRIL

May the glad dawn
Of Easter morn
Bring joy to thee.
May the calm eve
Of Easter leave
A peace divine with thee.
May Easter night,
On thine heart write,
O Christ I live for Thee.

UNKNOWN

LIVING A NEW LIFE
Quiet Times, New Gifts

Fifteen years ago in the dead of winter, my wife, Barbara, and I bought a little farm in Texas. We loved the tiny yellow house, the faded red barn, and the spring-fed creek, and we could picture how lush the pastures would soon be. But springtime only brought waist-high weeds. The county agent suggested that we plow the weeds under and plant Coastal Bermuda, a popular grass in the area.

Our neighbor had a better idea. "Go with the native grasses that God put there," he advised. We followed his advice, and by the fall, we counted more than twenty different kinds of grass, including the prized bluestem, which had sustained the buffalo grazing there a century before.

Last summer, a mild stroke forced me to cancel my speaking and teaching responsibilities for the year. I discovered that the principle my neighbor had suggested for our pasture also worked for my life. Previously, I would rise early for overly full days and nights of preaching and pastoring, or heading for the airport for a week of speaking. Now I sit quietly each morning, reading for an hour in my handmade rocking chair. With the heavy activities cut back, my soul is being fed, and I have time to explore a variety of other gifts. And I thank God for the new opportunities to grow.

—*Kenneth Chafin*

APRIL 2026

SUNDAY	MONDAY	TUESDAY	WEDNESDAY	THURSDAY	FRIDAY	SATURDAY
			1 PASSOVER BEGINS AT SUNDOWN	2 MAUNDY THURSDAY	3 GOOD FRIDAY	4
5 EASTER	6	7	8	9	10	11
12	13	14	15	16	17	18
19	20	21	22 EARTH DAY	23	27	28
26	27	28	29	30		

NOTES

MARCH

S	M	T	W	T	F	S
1	2	3	4	5	6	7
8	9	10	11	12	13	14
15	16	17	18	19	20	21
22	23	24	25	26	27	28
29	30	31				

MAY

S	M	T	W	T	F	S
					1	2
3	4	5	6	7	8	9
10	11	12	13	14	15	16
17	18	19	20	21	22	23
24/31	25	26	27	28	29	30

GUIDEPOSTS DAILY PLANNER

OUR PRAYER
Dear God, help me always to see beyond my fears to the beauty of Your creation.

29
SUNDAY
PALM SUNDAY

Go into the village ahead of you, and immediately as you enter it, you will find tied there a colt that has never been ridden; untie it and bring it. If anyone says to you, "Why are you doing this?" just say this: "The Lord needs it and will send it back here immediately." —Mark 11:2–3 (NRSVUE)

30
MONDAY

Start children off on the way they should go, and even when they are old they will not turn from it. —Proverbs 22:6 (NIV)

31
TUESDAY

So do not throw away your confidence; it will be richly rewarded. —Hebrews 10:35 (NIV)

My eight-year-old son, Michael, recently stood in the middle of the kitchen and kissed a bee. It was about the size of a jellybean, in a yellow and black body.

I've always had such a fear of bees that the very thought of kissing one sent me shrieking. "Michael!" I shouted. "What are you doing? Are you crazy?"

My son gave me a look of hurt and surprise.

"I kissed the bee. I showed everyone in school how I kiss a bee."

"But it can sting you," I said with my adult voice of knowing.

"Daddy, the bee is dead. It's cute too. Look how little it is."

I bent down for a close look at the bee curled in Michael's small palm. It had a certain charm about it, I'll admit.

APRIL

1 WEDNESDAY
PASSOVER BEGINS AT SUNDOWN

. . . thy wondrous works declare. —Psalm 75:1 (KJV)

2 THURSDAY
MAUNDY THURSDAY

Then [Jesus] took a loaf of bread, and when he had given thanks he broke it and gave it to them, saying, "This is my body, which is given for you. Do this in remembrance of me." —Luke 22:19 (NRSVUE)

3 FRIDAY
GOOD FRIDAY

When it was noon, darkness came over the whole land until three in the afternoon. At three o'clock Jesus cried out with a loud voice, "Eloi, Eloi, lema sabachthani?" which means, "My God, my God, why have you forsaken me?" —Mark 15:33–34 (NRSVUE)

4 SATURDAY

They took the body of Jesus and wrapped it with the spices in linen cloths, according to the burial custom of the Jews. —John 19:40 (NRSVUE)

Children often lead us to simple truths that we sometimes forget. Thanks to Michael, I had seen the beauty of one of God's creatures that previously I had only feared.

—*Christopher de Vinck*

PRAYER REQUESTS _____

APRIL

S	M	T	W	T	F	S
			1	2	3	4
5	6	7	8	9	10	11
12	13	14	15	16	17	18
19	20	21	22	23	24	25
26	27	28	29	30		

OUR PRAYER

*Help me always to thank You for all things,
even before I see You at work.*

---

5 **SUNDAY** **EASTER** — If we died with Christ, we believe that we will also live with him. —Romans 6:8 (NRSVUE)

---

6 **MONDAY** — Very truly, I tell you, you will weep and mourn, but the world will rejoice; you will have pain, but your pain will turn into joy. —John 16:20 (NRSVUE)

---

7 **TUESDAY** — Lord, you establish peace for us; all that we have accomplished you have done for us. —Isaiah 26:12 (NIV)

I STEPPED OUT on my deck Easter Sunday morning a few years ago in Nashville, Tennessee, and looked out over the woods below just beginning to turn green. But not even the welcome signs of spring could make me ignore the untidiness below me. The boy across the street hadn't come to mow the grass when he said he would. So the grass in my sloping backyard seemed at least a foot high and was beginning to go to seed. I had wanted the lawn to be neat for Easter, and I was provoked at him that it wasn't.

Just as I turned to go inside, something bright blue in the tall grass caught my eye. *More untidiness*, I thought with annoyance. *Something one of the neighborhood dogs dragged over and left.* Just as I started down the stairs to pick it up and dispose of it, I recognized it. A bird! An indigo bunting! In my yard. Feeding on the seeds in my uncut, untidy grass.

I had been hardening my heart because of my neighbor boy's negligence and my resulting unkempt lawn. *Easter should be celebrated with neatness*, I had felt. But God was telling me that He celebrated Easter with new life, and life is prolific, abundant—

8
WEDNESDAY

Everything is possible for one who believes. —Mark 9:23 (NIV)

9
THURSDAY

May our sons in their youth be like plants full grown, our daughters like corner pillars. —Psalm 144:12 (NRSVCE)

10
FRIDAY

Always take time to talk to God. Put your mind on what you are saying. And thank God for what he has done. —Colossians 4:2 (WE)

11
SATURDAY

Both the one who makes people holy and those who are made holy are of the same family. —Hebrews 2:11 (NIV)

APRIL

---

not carefully boxed, landscaped, arranged.

I watched the indigo bunting and its more soberly colored mate feed on my abundant seeds. How grateful I was that the boy across the street had not cut my grass.

—*Mary Ruth Howes*

PRAYER REQUESTS _____

_____

_____

_____

APRIL

S	M	T	W	T	F	S
			1	2	3	4
5	6	7	8	9	10	11
12	13	14	15	16	17	18
19	20	21	22	23	24	25
26	27	28	29	30		

GUIDEPOSTS DAILY PLANNER

OUR PRAYER
Truly, Lord, the greatest thing in the world is loving You!

---

12 SUNDAY — Remember the long way that the Lord your God has made you travel. —Deuteronomy 8:2 (JPS)

---

13 MONDAY — Walk with the wise and become wise. —Proverbs 13:20 (NIV)

---

14 TUESDAY — The Lord is my shepherd; I shall not want. He maketh me to lie down in green pastures: he leadeth me beside the still waters. —Psalm 23:1–2 (KJV)

As I registered for the weekend retreat at Canyon Meadows in the Southern California mountains, I was handed a small package wrapped in a dainty floral print. "When you get to your room," the young woman told me, "please unwrap this and read the label first thing." Her eyes danced as she looked at my quizzical expression.

I did as she said—first thing—and found a small baby-food jar filled with grains of rice and one fairly large walnut. The label read:

The walnut in this jar represents the time we spend with God. The rice represents the time we spend doing other things. If you pour the rice into the jar first, then try to insert the walnut, it will not fit. If you put the walnut in first, then pour the rice around it, there is a perfect fit.

Likewise, if we spend time doing other things first, we will never find time to spend with God. If we spend time with God first, there will always be time for other things.

No wonder my week had been so frantic and

15
WEDNESDAY

His purpose was for the nations to seek after God and perhaps feel their way toward him and find him—though he is not far from any one of us. —Acts 17:27 (NLT)

16
THURSDAY

The LORD is near to all who call on him. —Psalm 145:18 (ESV)

17
FRIDAY

When I called, you answered me. —Psalm 138:3 (NIV)

18
SATURDAY

See the way God does things and fall into line. Don't fight the facts of nature. —Ecclesiastes 7:13 (TLB)

---

out of whack. I had filled my hours with errands, phone calls, housework, and paperwork, until there was no room for time with God. There and then I made a new commitment: "Every single day, dear Lord, the walnut goes in first!"

—*Fay Angus*

PRAYER REQUESTS

APRIL

S	M	T	W	T	F	S
			1	2	3	4
5	6	7	8	9	10	11
12	13	14	15	16	17	18
19	20	21	22	23	24	25
26	27	28	29	30		

OUR PRAYER

Loving Father, help me to recognize, and even welcome, lessons in patience.

---

19 SUNDAY — O Lord, our Lord, how excellent is thy name in all the earth! who hast set thy glory above the heavens. —Psalm 8:1 (KJV)

---

20 MONDAY — [Jesus] would withdraw to deserted places to pray. —Luke 5:16 (NABRE)

---

21 TUESDAY — We have many parts in the one body, and all these parts have different functions. —Romans 12:4 (GNT)

"When will the well-drillers be here?" I asked my husband as he hung up the phone.

"Toward the end of the week. They're being delayed by equipment breakdowns," Harry replied.

"That's the same thing they've told us for the last three weeks," I complained as I heated a pot of water for washing the breakfast dishes.

"Look," Harry said, "this is going to get the best of us. What can we find in this situation that's good? What do you think God might want to teach us here?"

As we explored it together, it didn't take long to see that this was a great opportunity for us to practice patience. That's not one of the things I'm famous for. I realized that I could continue to complain, or I could accept the situation and ask God to "grow" patience in me, and maybe even a cheerful attitude about the inconvenience. And so it was that Harry and I went to work at being patient.

The well-drillers finally did come, and we were grateful to find good water at a reasonable depth. Now we're getting into the serious house-building stage, and I can almost see our heavenly Father saying

APRIL 2026

22
WEDNESDAY
EARTH DAY

Consider the lilies how they grow: they toil not, they spin not; and yet I say unto you, that Solomon in all his glory was not arrayed like one of these. —Luke 12:27 (KJV)

23
THURSDAY

All their neighbors assisted them. —Ezra 1:6 (NIV)

24
FRIDAY

If you falter in a time of trouble, how small is your strength! —Proverbs 24:10 (NIV)

25
SATURDAY

Make allowance for each other's faults, and forgive anyone who offends you. —Colossians 3:13 (NLT)

---

with a smile, "Just look at all these opportunities I'll be giving you to practice that patience thing: delays in the building permit process, waiting for the concrete truck or the plumber or the electrician..." Thank You, Lord. We can hardly wait.

—*Mary Jane Clark*

PRAYER REQUESTS _____
_____
_____
_____

APRIL

S	M	T	W	T	F	S
			1	2	3	4
5	6	7	8	9	10	11
12	13	14	15	16	17	18
19	20	21	22	23	24	25
26	27	28	29	30		

GUIDEPOSTS DAILY PLANNER

OUR PRAYER
Father, may I have the faith to allow my family into the people You created them to be.

---

26 SUNDAY

For the L ORD is good; His mercy is everlasting and His faithfulness is to all generations. —Psalm 100:5 (NASB)

---

27 MONDAY

Whoever fears the L ORD has a secure fortress, and for their children it will be a refuge. —Proverbs 14:26 (NIV)

---

28 TUESDAY

God brought Abram outside beneath the nighttime sky and told him, "Look up into the heavens and count the stars if you can. Your descendants will be like that—too many to count!" —Genesis 15:5 (TLB)

"WHAT DO YOU WANT for graduation, Derek?" I asked our 22-year-old son as our family ate lunch together in a campus cafeteria. I expected a sensible answer like "a watch," or something silly and extravagant like "a million dollars." I wasn't prepared for his real answer.

"An ice ax," he said, without hesitation, as if he'd already thought about it. Immediately, I pictured him climbing the mountains he loved, burying an axe into a glacier—and then slipping and falling.

After lunch, we headed off to the store, where Derek began examining a variety of axes. I shuddered just looking at them, but then I became curious about the different sizes and shapes.

"What's the difference?" I asked Derek.

"Some are mountaineering ice axes and some are climbing axes, so it depends on the use and height and weight of the climber," he explained.

Surprised, I looked at him with a new sense of respect. How did this child of mine know so much about something so unknown and scary to me?

Finally, Derek selected one, and I held it as we stood in line to pay for it, asking God to bless it

29
WEDNESDAY

Praise the Lord, my soul, and forget not all his benefits. —Psalm 103:2 (NIV)

30
THURSDAY

Return to your rest, my soul. —Psalm 116:7 (NASB)

MAY 1
FRIDAY

Therefore keep watch, because you do not know the day or the hour. —Matthew 25:13 (NIV)

2
SATURDAY

Confess your sins to each other and pray for each other so that you may be healed. The prayer of a righteous person is powerful and effective. —James 5:16 (NIV)

---

and use it as a tool to protect and anchor Derek on all his future adventures. "Happy graduation!" I said, when I handed it over to him.

"How'd you know this is just what I wanted?" he grinned.

—*Carol Kuykendall*

PRAYER REQUESTS _____

APRIL

S	M	T	W	T	F	S
			1	2	3	4
5	6	7	8	9	10	11
12	13	14	15	16	17	18
19	20	21	22	23	24	25
26	27	28	29	30		

GUIDEPOSTS DAILY PLANNER

You hold fast my to My name . . . —REVELATION 2:13 (NKJV)

A PRAYER FOR MAY

Incline us oh God! to think
humbly of ourselves,
to be severe
only in the examination
of our own conduct,
to consider
our fellow creatures
with kindness,
and to judge
of all they say
and do
with that charity
which we would desire
from them ourselves.

JANE AUSTEN (1775–1817)

LIVING A NEW LIFE
Graduation Day?

At the beginning of May I was on top of the world and preparing to graduate from the University of Tennessee. Until, five days before graduation . . .

"Brock, I've been trying to call you," my adviser said, worried. "There's been a goof-up. You're two hours short of meeting graduation requirements."

"What? How could this possibly happen?"

"Listen, I'm going to meet with the department head and see if we can work something out. Our only hope is last summer's internship. If you could write a paper relating it to your major, there's a possibility the university will give you the hours you need."

For two days I lived in the library. The only breaks I took were to eat and to update my family. "You're going to make it, Brock!" my sister, Keri, encouraged me.

On the eve of graduation, the call came. "Congratulations, Brock. You did it." I never felt so relieved. I made the call to my family to let them know they could come to see me receive my diploma after all.

"We're packed and ready," they told me, laughing.

The next morning, in cap and gown, I walked into Thompson-Boling Arena, grateful for a caring adviser, a supportive family, and, most important, a God who answers prayers, all working together to help me get here.

—*Brock Kidd*

MAY 2026

SUNDAY	MONDAY	TUESDAY	WEDNESDAY	THURSDAY	FRIDAY	SATURDAY
					1	2
3	4	5	6	7 NATIONAL DAY OF PRAYER	8	9
10 MOTHER'S DAY	11	12	13	14 ASCENSION DAY	15	16
17	18	19	20	21	22	23
24 PENTECOST / 31	25 MEMORIAL DAY	26	27	28	29	30

NOTES

APRIL

S	M	T	W	T	F	S
			1	2	3	4
5	6	7	8	9	10	11
12	13	14	15	16	17	18
19	20	21	22	23	24	25
26	27	28	29	30		

JUNE

S	M	T	W	T	F	S
	1	2	3	4	5	6
7	8	9	10	11	12	13
14	15	16	17	18	19	20
21	22	23	24	25	26	27
28	29	30				

GUIDEPOSTS DAILY PLANNER

OUR PRAYER
Lord, in all my attitudes, keep me facing toward You.

---

3 SUNDAY

The earth is the Lord's. —Psalm 24:1 (KJV)

---

4 MONDAY

But the word of the Lord came to me [David], saying, Thou hast shed blood abundantly, and . . . shalt not build a house unto my name. —1 Chronicles 22:8 (KJV)

---

5 TUESDAY

So faith comes from hearing, and hearing through the word of Christ. —Romans 10:17 (ESV)

"Attitudes," a great American psychiatrist once said, "are more important than facts." I thought of this the other day when I went to see a longtime friend in the hospital. Jack had been a marvelous athlete as a young man and an energetic civic leader in the years that followed. Now the sudden onset of a serious kidney disorder had left him dependent on dialysis machines just to stay alive.

I knew how difficult this drastically curtailed existence must be for him and tried to express the sympathy I felt. But he waved my words aside. "We all go through stages in life," he said. "Here I am, and I can't say I enjoy these surroundings. What I try to focus on is the fun I've had getting here. The Lord gave me so many good times that there's no end to the happy memories I can summon up. When I do, this hospital room just fades away."

The fun I've had getting here. I wish I had a

6 WEDNESDAY

Finally, brothers and sisters, whatever is true, whatever is noble, whatever is right, whatever is pure, whatever is lovely, whatever is admirable—if anything is excellent or praiseworthy—think about such things. —Philippians 4:8 (NIV)

7 THURSDAY
NATIONAL DAY OF PRAYER

Commit to the Lord whatever you do, and he will establish your plans. —Proverbs 16:3 (NIV)

8 FRIDAY

Peter came and said to him, "Lord, if my brother or sister sins against me, how often should I forgive? As many as seven times?" Jesus said to him, "Not seven times, but, I tell you, seventy-seven times." —Matthew 18:21–22 (NRSVUE)

9 SATURDAY

A certain Samaritan . . . when he saw him, he had compassion on him. —Luke 10:33 (KJV)

---

calendar with that phrase inscribed at the top of every page. Even on dark days, it would be a reminder of how many sunny ones there have been. A reminder, too, to be grateful to the One who made those happy times possible.

—*Arthur Gordon*

PRAYER REQUESTS

MAY

S	M	T	W	T	F	S
					1	2
3	4	5	6	7	8	9
10	11	12	13	14	15	16
17	18	19	20	21	22	23
24/31	25	26	27	28	29	30

OUR PRAYER
Lord Jesus, brighten my desire to love others in everyday ways.

10 SUNDAY — MOTHER'S DAY
But I am like an olive tree flourishing in the house of God; I trust in God's unfailing love for ever and ever. —Psalm 52:8 (NIV)

11 MONDAY
Weeping may endure for a night, but joy comes in the morning. —Psalm 30:5 (NKJV)

12 TUESDAY
You did not choose me, but I chose you and appointed you so that you might go and bear fruit. —John 15:16 (NIV)

I ONCE HEARD another woman describe motherhood in three words: "Laundry, laundry, laundry!" I had to laugh because, having given birth to four children in four-and-a-half years, I always had such a huge pile of clothes beside the washing machine that I called it my "mountaintop experience."

Over the years, I've managed to pull some amusing—and heroic—memories from my laundry basket. There was the time, when the children were small, that I got so far behind on the washing, my husband packed me off to my mother's while he stayed home with the kids and did sixteen loads of clothes. (Now that's heroic!) One time we had a mouse in our basement, and I would load the clothes in a flurry, stamping my feet the whole time and singing at the top of my lungs! When the kids grew into teenagers, the big joke was the record ninety-eight socks without mates that we counted one day!

My clothes-washing days are on slow spin now as the kids go out the door much the way they came in—one after another. And one place where I particularly feel their absence is the laundry room. I miss those wash-and-wear traces of their

13
WEDNESDAY

He answered and said unto them, Because it is given unto you to know the mysteries of the kingdom of heaven, but to them it is not given. —Matthew 13:11 (KJV)

14
THURSDAY
ASCENSION DAY

How long will you grieve my spirit, and crush me with words? —Job 19:2 (JPS)

15
FRIDAY

Where two or three are gathered in my name, I am there among them. —Matthew 18:20 (NRSVUE)

16
SATURDAY

A person of too many friends comes to ruin, but there is a friend who sticks closer than a brother. —Proverbs 18:24 (NASB)

MAY

nearness—the loud green socks, the number nine volleyball uniform, the handmade blue skirt.

My laundry room view may have seemed a little hazy some days, but having those kids around to love in everyday ways truly was a "mountaintop experience."

—*Carol Knapp*

PRAYER REQUESTS _____

MAY

S	M	T	W	T	F	S
					1	2
3	4	5	6	7	8	9
10	11	12	13	14	15	16
17	18	19	20	21	22	23
24/31	25	26	27	28	29	30

GUIDEPOSTS DAILY PLANNER

OUR PRAYER

*Today, Lord, bless this place and time that
I've set aside to be with You.*

17
SUNDAY

There is a time for everything, and a season for every activity under the heavens.
—Ecclesiastes 3:1 (NIV)

18
MONDAY

Follow God's example, therefore, as dearly loved children and walk in the way of love, just as Christ loved us and gave himself up for us as a fragrant offering and sacrifice to God. —Ephesians 5:1–2 (NIV)

19
TUESDAY

Encourage each other. —2 Corinthians 13:11 (NLT)

It's 7 o'clock on a May morning, seventy degrees in Oak Creek, Wisconsin. I'm sitting in a very comfortable yellow rocker on my deck with a large mug of Earl Grey tea. Two squirrels are dining on the ear of corn attached to the "squirrel diner" at the end of the deck, and a dozen birds are singing their way through breakfast, also provided by the management.

This deck is my place and time for prayer. No newspapers, books, people, or phone calls. Just me, the birds, squirrels, and God.

Morning prayers were part of my life as a child. But then in college and into marriage and motherhood, my morning prayers fell by the wayside. Twenty-five years passed.

Then one spring, I discovered how quiet and peaceful it was on my deck in the early morning, and I began to pray. I thanked God for this place of beauty and this hour of quiet and for this wonderful chair I found at a yard sale. I praised Him for the trees—and asked Him for many favors.

Do you have a specific place and a definite time for morning prayer? Believe me, it's an amazing way to start your day. It calms you, keeps your life

20
WEDNESDAY

He is like a tree planted by water, that sends out its roots by the stream, and does not fear when heat comes, for its leaves remain green, and is not anxious in the year of drought, for it does not cease to bear fruit. —Jeremiah 17:8 (ESV)

21
THURSDAY

For every house is built by someone, but God is the builder of everything. —Hebrews 3:4 (NIV)

22
FRIDAY

Do you not know that in a race all the runners run, but only one receives the prize? So run that you may obtain it. —1 Corinthians 9:24 (ESV)

23
SATURDAY

In all things you yourself must be an example of good behavior. —Titus 2:7 (GNT)

MAY

focused, reminds you of what's truly important and begins each day on a positive, happy note. Promise yourself thirty minutes alone in your favorite spot every morning. Bring a cup of tea or coffee and perhaps the book of Psalms to get you started.

—*Patricia Lorenz*

PRAYER REQUESTS _____

_____

_____

MAY

S	M	T	W	T	F	S
					1	2
3	4	5	6	7	8	9
10	11	12	13	14	15	16
17	18	19	20	21	22	23
24/31	25	26	27	28	29	30

GUIDEPOSTS DAILY PLANNER

OUR PRAYER

Forgive me for bothering You about my imperfection, Lord. It seemed important at the time.

---

24 SUNDAY — PENTECOST

[Jesus] said to them, "Cast the net on the right-hand side of the boat and you will find the fish." —John 21:6 (NASB)

---

25 MONDAY — MEMORIAL DAY

Now therefore, our God, we thank You and praise Your glorious name. —1 Chronicles 29:13 (NKJV)

---

26 TUESDAY

He who forms the hearts of all, who considers everything they do. —Psalm 33:15 (NIV)

I was in my early teens before I knew about one of my imperfections. I'd just appeared in a school play and believed I'd done pretty well because several people said so. That included one woman who told my mother authoritatively that I showed great potential as an actor, but, of course, something would have to be done about "his lisp."

There are two things I'd never thought about: (1) becoming an actor; (2) my having a lisp. Nobody had mentioned it to me before. But from then on I was always aware of it. In our daily chapel at school, I'd often ask God to do something about it. The best He seemed to do was to have people tell me they hardly noticed it. I didn't believe them.

God did do something, however. Some years ago, forced to make a speech I'd tried to avoid, I began my talk with an attempt to disarm my listeners by saying, "The terrible thing about a lisp is you can't say it without doing it." Later, a man came up to me and said, "You haven't accepted that lisp of yours, have you?"

I was so surprised by his directness that I could only nod. "A wise man once told me," he went on, "if you accept your limitations, you go beyond them. Think about it."

27
WEDNESDAY

The God of all grace, who called you to his eternal glory in Christ, after you have suffered a little while, will himself restore you and make you strong, firm, and steadfast. —1 Peter 5:10 (NIV)

28
THURSDAY

Pride goes before destruction, a haughty spirit before a fall. —Proverbs 16:18 (NIV)

29
FRIDAY

"Do not be afraid. Stand still, and see the salvation of the LORD, which He will accomplish for you today." —Exodus 14:13 (NKJV)

30
SATURDAY

Grandchildren are the crown of the elderly. —Proverbs 17:6 (CSB)

Think about it I did.

So today, if there's anybody reading this who'd like me to come and speak, I'm available. But fair warning: You, too, will have to accept my limitations.

—*Van Varner*

PRAYER REQUESTS _____

MAY

S	M	T	W	T	F	S
					1	2
3	4	5	6	7	8	9
10	11	12	13	14	15	16
17	18	19	20	21	22	23
24/31	25	26	27	28	29	30

GUIDEPOSTS DAILY PLANNER

We are fools for Christ's sake . . . —1 CORINTHIANS 4:10 (NKJV)

LIVING A NEW LIFE
Clowning for God

It's Sunday morning and I'm sitting on an old tub in the furnace room of our church, wearing an orange and purple clown suit. I am to make a surprise appearance in the sanctuary to promote Vacation Bible School as Rosco, the VBS mascot.

This is my very first time at clowning, and I am struggling with stage fright—and niggling questions about propriety: Will a middle-aged deacon's wife breach long-established ideas of decorum in our conservative church and alienate the parents she's hoping to reach?

Filtering down through the air duct comes the hymn "Take Time to Be Holy." Lyrics I never really heard before strike me: "Make friends of God's children." Isn't that what I intend to do in my colorful costume? Saying a quick prayer, I gather my props, adjust my huge bow tie, and waddle up the stairs into the sanctuary.

For a moment, the congregation is silent. Then, one by one, wide-eyed children begin to giggle, and somber adults cannot suppress amused grins. At the suggestion that perhaps nobody has time for Vacation Bible School, Rosco cries with disappointment, dabbing at his eyes with a huge red handkerchief. "So who will come and make Rosco happy?" asks the minister. Much to my surprise, everybody in the congregation raises a hand, and Rosco merrily exits, stage right.

—*Alma Barkman*

A PRAYER FOR JUNE

Could we with ink the ocean fill,
and were the skies of parchment made,
were every stalk on earth a quill,
and every man a scribe by trade,
to write the love of God above,
would drain the ocean dry.
Nor could the scroll contain the whole,
though stretched from sky to sky.

ADAPTED FROM "THE LOVE OF GOD"
BY FREDERICK LEHMAN

JUNE 2026

SUNDAY	MONDAY	TUESDAY	WEDNESDAY	THURSDAY	FRIDAY	SATURDAY
	1	2	3	4	5	6
7	8	9	10	11	12	13
14 FLAG DAY	15	16	17	18	19 JUNETEENTH	20
21 FATHER'S DAY SUMMER BEGINS	22	23	24	25	26	27
28	29	30				

NOTES

MAY

S	M	T	W	T	F	S
					1	2
3	4	5	6	7	8	9
10	11	12	13	14	15	16
17	18	19	20	21	22	23
24/31	25	26	27	28	29	30

JULY

S	M	T	W	T	F	S
			1	2	3	4
5	6	7	8	9	10	11
12	13	14	15	16	17	18
19	20	21	22	23	24	25
26	27	28	29	30	31	

GUIDEPOSTS DAILY PLANNER

OUR PRAYER
Dear God, today let me open my heart to the blessings I have all around me.

31 SUNDAY
Be strong in the Lord, and in the power of His might. Put on the whole armor of God, that you may be able to stand against the wiles of the devil. —Ephesians 6:10–11 (NKJV)

JUNE 1 MONDAY
. . . freely give. —Matthew 10:8 (KJV)

2 TUESDAY
In your unfailing love you will lead the people you have redeemed. —Exodus 15:13 (NIV)

LATELY, I HAVE BEEN READING about people who have had near-death experiences, and I must admit that I feel envious of the heavenly encounters they describe. You see, when I was 17 years old, I had open-heart surgery to repair a birth defect. I didn't come close to dying. I didn't see any angels or heard any harp music. But I did see Dr. Torres, who explained to me what the operation would entail. My boyfriend at the time came to visit me at the hospital every single day; so did my closest friend and my mother. Six girls from a school club that I belonged to had taken the club dues and, instead of going out for a big lunch, bought me a delicate gold locket with "Love" engraved on the back.

A friend to whom I related this just chuckled. "Sounds like you had something better than a near-death experience. You had an open-heart experience. You got to see that you had friends who cared enough to send you cards and come to see you, relatives who rallied around you, and a caring

3
WEDNESDAY

Carry each other's burdens, and in this way you will fulfill the law of Christ.
—Galatians 6:2 (NIV)

4
THURSDAY

Everything they do is done for people to see. —Matthew 23:5 (NIV)

5
FRIDAY

You make known to me the path of life; you will fill me with joy in your presence, with eternal pleasures at your right hand. —Psalm 16:11 (NIV)

6
SATURDAY

May there be abundant grain throughout the land, flourishing even on the hilltops. —Psalm 72:16 (NLT)

---

doctor who took the time to explain everything to a frightened 17-year-old girl."

After a moment, I touched my friend's hand.

"And I have a friend who cares enough to remind me to focus on what's important in life—my blessings!"

—*Linda Neukrug*

PRAYER REQUESTS _____

_____

_____

_____

JUNE

S	M	T	W	T	F	S
	1	2	3	4	5	6
7	8	9	10	11	12	13
14	15	16	17	18	19	20
21	22	23	24	25	26	27
28	29	30				

GUIDEPOSTS DAILY PLANNER

OUR PRAYER

Loving Father, please forgive me for _____.

---

7 SUNDAY

I consider that the sufferings of this present time are not worth comparing with the glory that is to be revealed to us. —Romans 8:18 (ESV)

---

8 MONDAY

In peace I will lie down and sleep, for you alone, LORD, make me dwell in safety. —Psalm 4:8 (NIV)

---

9 TUESDAY

"Well done, good and faithful servant!" —Matthew 25:23 (NIV)

I MUST HAVE BEEN seven or eight when I knocked my father's expensive camera off the table in his "off-limits" basement darkroom. When I picked up the camera, the lens fell to pieces. *Uh-oh! What in the world am I going to do?* I was scared to death of my father's loud voice and angry words, but most of all, I was afraid of losing his love. I decided not to tell him.

That night I prayed, "God, please don't let Daddy find out I broke his camera." It didn't help a bit. I still felt like a terrible child. Then God's answer came with the urgent thought: *Go tell him.* I fought it as long as I could, but then I forced myself to get up. Daddy was sitting in his big chair by the fireplace reading a book.

When he finally looked up, my knees were shaking and tears were running down my face. "I broke your camera!" I blurted.

He stared at me, then lectured me about disobeying him and grounded me for the weekend. Next, he did a surprising thing. He reached into his pocket and handed me a dollar and said, "This is for telling the truth." Then Daddy lifted me into his lap and held me tight until I fell asleep in his arms.

10 WEDNESDAY

So be truly glad. There is wonderful joy ahead, even though you must endure many trials for a little while. —1 Peter 1:6 (NLT)

11 THURSDAY

You anoint my head with oil; my cup overflows. —Psalm 23:5 (NIV)

12 FRIDAY

The seed falling on good soil refers to someone who hears the word and understands it. This is the one who produces a crop, yielding a hundred, sixty or thirty times what was sown. —Matthew 13:23 (NIV)

13 SATURDAY

Then the word of the LORD came to Elijah: "Leave here, turn eastward . . . I have directed the ravens to supply you with food there." . . . The ravens brought him bread and meat in the morning and bread and meat in the evening. —1 Kings 17:2–4, 6 (NIV)

Even now, whenever I feel guilty, I think of that dollar, that soft lap, those loving arms. And I remember that when I confess my faults to my heavenly Father, He also rewards me—not with money, but with a peaceful heart and His loving arms.

—*Marilyn Morgan Helleberg*

PRAYER REQUESTS _____

_____

_____

_____

JUNE

S	M	T	W	T	F	S
	1	2	3	4	5	6
7	8	9	10	11	12	13
14	15	16	17	18	19	20
21	22	23	24	25	26	27
28	29	30				

OUR PRAYER
Lord, make me worthy of the faith others have in me, and strong enough to bear faith's burdens.

---

14 SUNDAY — FLAG DAY

The one who was dying blessed me. —Job 29:13 (NIV)

---

15 MONDAY

All of you who were baptized into Christ have clothed yourselves with Christ. —Galatians 3:27 (NIV)

---

16 TUESDAY

Do not seek revenge or bear a grudge against anyone among your people, but love your neighbor as yourself. I am the Lord. —Leviticus 19:18 (NIV)

My grandfather is good at "keeping at." Though 87, he still tends his family's cemetery plots, old graves that lie in an even older cemetery in Mount Greenwood, Illinois. I often volunteer to drive him on his rounds and cannot help being awed by his faithful commitment to his family and to honoring their memory.

I stand back and watch him as he tends the family memorials. He strides about, a wistful look on his craggy face, weeding and clipping as he goes. While he works, I notice he stands more erect, his pace quicker, his every action vital and purposeful. Bending agilely, he plucks a nettle from the grass crowding a small, weathered stone reading simply, "Martha Mutzbauer—Beloved Sister." He doesn't forget Martha, who passed away when he was three. He promised his parents he wouldn't.

Driving home from the cemetery one day, "Pa" sat quietly, a contented, fulfilled look on his face. After reading in silence for a while, he seemed to search for the right words, then said to me earnestly, "Y'know, Jen, I'd like geraniums on my plot when my time comes. They sure do last the summer, don't they?"

His abruptness and the thought of his passing

17
WEDNESDAY

You undid my sackcloth and girded me with joy. —Psalm 30:12 (JPS)

18
THURSDAY

Every time I think of you, I give thanks to my God. —Philippians 1:3 (NLT)

19
FRIDAY
JUNETEENTH

Let us not become weary in doing good, for at the proper time we will reap a harvest if we do not give up. —Galatians 6:9 (NIV)

20
SATURDAY

Beware of practicing your righteousness before other people in order to be seen by them, for then you will have no reward from your Father who is in heaven. —Matthew 6:1 (ESV)

---

made me uncomfortable, and I teased, "Pa, if I get to be rich and famous, how do you know I'll even have time to visit, much less plant geraniums?"

He didn't miss a beat. He simply patted my knee and said, "You won't forget, Jen."

—*Jenny Mutzbauer*

PRAYER REQUESTS _____

JUNE

S	M	T	W	T	F	S
	1	2	3	4	5	6
7	8	9	10	11	12	13
14	15	16	17	18	19	20
21	22	23	24	25	26	27
28	29	30				

OUR PRAYER
Father, please help me daily to position Your Word front and center.

---

21 SUNDAY
FATHER'S DAY
SUMMER BEGINS

Father of the fatherless and protector of widows is God in his holy habitation. —Psalm 68:5 (ESV)

---

22 MONDAY

What a person desires is unfailing love. —Proverbs 19:22 (NIV)

---

23 TUESDAY

My eyes are awake before the watches of the night, that I may meditate on your promise. —Psalm 119:148 (ESV)

IDEALLY, I LIKE TO BEGIN my day in my office at home with Bible reading and prayer. But yesterday, when my working day came to an end, my Bible had not been opened. It was buried beneath the details of one project after another that needed to be handled immediately.

That evening on a TV nature show, I found my answer. The screen came to life just in time for me to see the tail of a desert mouse disappearing into its sandy burrow for the night. Once inside, the mouse closed the hole behind it by deftly pulling a small stone across the opening. "You've just witnessed a nightly, routine performance," the narrator explained. "The pebble neatly camouflages the entrance to keep out any predators.

"But the stone serves another purpose," the narrator continued. "As the hot desert air cools off during the night, a single drop of dew condenses on the surface of the stone. In the morning, just as the sun begins to rise, the thirsty mouse emerges from its dark burrow to drink that one life-giving drop of precious water. It's enough fluid to carry the tiny creature through another day of dry, searing heat."

Such mouse ingenuity gave me an idea. Before

24
WEDNESDAY

I thank Christ Jesus . . . because He considered me faithful, putting me into service.
—1 Timothy 1:12 (NASB)

25
THURSDAY

Thanks be to God, who gives us the victory through our Lord Jesus Christ.
—1 Corinthians 15:57 (ESV)

26
FRIDAY

Think of the kindness you wish others would show you; do the same for them.
—Luke 6:31 (VOICE)

27
SATURDAY

For who has despised the day of small things? —Zechariah 4:10 (NKJV)

JUNE

going to bed, I went downstairs to my office and thumbed through my Bible until I located the passage listed for today's date in my daily reading guide. Then I positioned the open Bible in a conspicuous place on my desk, ready to receive its life-giving water in the morning.

—*Alma Barkman*

PRAYER REQUESTS

JUNE

S	M	T	W	T	F	S
	1	2	3	4	5	6
7	8	9	10	11	12	13
14	15	16	17	18	19	20
21	22	23	24	25	26	27
28	29	30				

GUIDEPOSTS DAILY PLANNER

Guideposts

Looking for a great gift idea?

Your search has ended! *Guideposts Daily Planner* makes a present that everyone on your holiday list will appreciate.

Guideposts Daily Planner offers you all of this and more!

- Organization at a glance
- Moving devotions to mark the passing months
- Spiral binding so your planner will lie flat
- A special place for prayer requests
- Encouraging Scripture verses to start each day

It's time to reserve your copy of Guideposts Daily Planner 2027!

IT'S EASY TO PREORDER:

1. Preorder by mail. Return the coupon with payment.
2. Preorder by phone. Call (800) 932-2145.

Orders accepted beginning August 1, 2026.

(RETURN PORTION OF THIS FORM WITH YOUR PAYMENT.)

PREORDER BY MAIL.

Please reserve my copy of *Guideposts Daily Planner 2027.*

Plus, I will be entitled to preview future editions of *Guideposts Daily Planner* at the then-current price with no obligation to purchase. I will always be notified in advance so I can decide if I want to preview the *Daily Planner* with no obligation whatsoever.

_____
Name (PLEASE PRINT)

_____
Address

_____
City   State   ZIP Code

Total copies reserved at $16.95 plus shipping and processing: _____

GPSGP014E75692NY

Please allow 4 weeks for delivery after your order is processed.

Mail this form to:
Guideposts
PO Box 5822
Harlan, Iowa 51593

Guideposts

"The kingdom of heaven is like a net that was let down into the lake and caught all kinds of fish." —MATTHEW 13:47 (NIV)

A PRAYER FOR JULY

I arise today,
Through the strength of Heaven;
Light of sun,
Brilliance of moon,
Splendor of fire,
Speed of lightning,
Swiftness of wind,
Depth of sea,
Stability of earth,
Firmness of rock.

ATTRIBUTED TO ST. PATRICK

LIVING A NEW LIFE
The Power of Acceptance

I had recently started a job as a supervisor in a research library. Although it seemed ideal in the beginning, it wasn't long before things began to fall apart. I found the office politics distasteful and, finally, I ended up resigning. But I could not easily let go of the disappointment. *Was I overbearing with the staff? Was I unprofessional?* I couldn't pin down what had gone wrong.

About that time, I bought my 5-year-old son, David, a fishing game. It came complete with a cardboard fishing tank, rods, sea creatures—a colorful sunfish, a sawfish, a dolphin, and a squid—plus other underwater objects like a tin can, an old boot, a bottle, and even a treasure chest.

One day, when David was "fishing," he snagged an old boot on his fishing line. "Another bad catch." He took the boot and threw it back into the tank. "I'll try again—for the sunfish this time." And he tossed his line in.

Then I saw it clearly: This job had simply been a "bad catch." In time I would find the right job. For now, I needed to let go of my tin cans of disappointment, my old boots of bitterness, and, instead, trust God to help me with my next "catch." With His help, it just may be a treasure of a job!

—*Robin White Goode*

JULY 2026

SUNDAY	MONDAY	TUESDAY	WEDNESDAY	THURSDAY	FRIDAY	SATURDAY
			1	2	3	4 INDEPENDENCE DAY
5	6	7	8	9	10	11
12	13	14	15	16	17	18
19	20	21	22	23	24	25
26	27	28	29	30	31	

NOTES

JUNE

S	M	T	W	T	F	S
	1	2	3	4	5	6
7	8	9	10	11	12	13
14	15	16	17	18	19	20
21	22	23	24	25	26	27
28	29	30				

AUGUST

S	M	T	W	T	F	S
						1
2	3	4	5	6	7	8
9	10	11	12	13	14	15
16	17	18	19	20	21	22
23/30	24/31	25	26	27	28	29

GUIDEPOSTS DAILY PLANNER

OUR PRAYER
Lord, make us wise enough to see that happiness comes when we follow the paths You showed us.

---

28 SUNDAY

Here I am! I stand at the door and knock. If anyone hears my voice and opens the door, I will come in and eat with that person, and they with me. —Revelation 3:20 (NIV)

---

29 MONDAY

Dear children, let us not love with words or speech but with actions and in truth. —1 John 3:18 (NIV)

---

30 TUESDAY

Further, my brothers and sisters, rejoice in the Lord! It is no trouble for me to write the same things to you again, and it is a safeguard for you. —Philippians 3:1 (NIV)

MY FATHER WAS A MAN who loved words and enjoyed finding new meanings in them. One Fourth of July, I remember, he was talking about that famous phrase from the Declaration of Independence: life, liberty, and the pursuit of happiness.

"I suppose we all do chase after happiness," he said. "But sometimes I wonder if it isn't the other way around. Maybe happiness is pursuing us. And if it never catches up, it may be because something is wrong in the way we're conducting our lives.

"I think the Lord wants us to be happy," my father went on, "and so He created a universe of mighty laws, both physical and spiritual. I've observed that a person is happy in proportion as he or she is in harmony with those laws. This means that if you want happiness to overtake you, you have to try to get rid of selfishness and dishonesty and anger and guilt and all the other roadblocks that keep it from catching up. When you clear those things out of your life and keep them out, you're giving

JUNE / JULY 2026

1
WEDNESDAY

Now, in my old age, don't set me aside. Don't forsake me now when my strength is failing. —Psalm 71:9 (TLB)

2
THURSDAY

Whoso keepeth his mouth and his tongue keepeth his soul from troubles. —Proverbs 21:23 (KJV)

3
FRIDAY

Speaking the truth in love, let us grow in every way into him who is the head—Christ. —Ephesians 4:15 (CSB)

4
SATURDAY
INDEPENDENCE DAY

Live as people who are free. —1 Peter 2:16 (ESV)

JULY

happiness a chance to come right up and tap you on the shoulder."

The pursuit of happiness. Is it catching up with you? Or is it falling behind? Something to think about now and then, I do believe.

—*Arthur Gordon*

PRAYER REQUESTS _____

JULY

S	M	T	W	T	F	S
			1	2	3	4
5	6	7	8	9	10	11
12	13	14	15	16	17	18
19	20	21	22	23	24	25
26	27	28	29	30	31	

GUIDEPOSTS DAILY PLANNER

OUR PRAYER

Dear Lord, I thank You for the people who help us make the best of everything.

5 SUNDAY
Oh, magnify the Lord with me, and let us exalt His name together. —Psalm 34:3 (NKJV)

6 MONDAY
I have loved you with an everlasting love. —Jeremiah 31:3 (NIV)

7 TUESDAY
Call unto me, and I will answer thee. —Jeremiah 33:3 (KJV)

Mama was the best doughnut maker in the whole wide world, and she made them frequently as I was growing up. But I remember one time in particular when she made a huge number of doughnuts. She put an especially beautiful red cloth on the table and lit two red candles. That evening she told us with a smile that she had decided to give us a "doughnut party," and we got to eat as many doughnuts as we wanted. There was nothing else for supper except freshly churned buttermilk.

Her smile and gay spirits were infectious, and I remember she was wearing a bright red apron and her coal-black hair was gleaming. There was a flame-like intensity about her.

Later, I happened to step quietly out onto our back porch, and I heard Mama saying to our father, "John, I do pray to God that we can sell some of that corn tomorrow, so that I can feed these young 'uns right. I just can't give them doughnuts again without truly making them sick."

So often over the years, I have thanked God for giving me a mother like that—one who made the best of what she had with a smile, and who in adversity always used her God-given imagination

JULY 2026

8
WEDNESDAY

The LORD is my shepherd; I have all that I need. —Psalm 23:1 (NLT)

9
THURSDAY

"You have heard that it was said, 'You shall love your neighbor and hate your enemy.' But I say to you, Love your enemies and pray for those who persecute you." —Matthew 5:43–44 (NRSVCE)

10
FRIDAY

Those the LORD has rescued will return. They will enter Zion with singing; everlasting joy will crown their heads. Gladness and joy will overtake them, and sorrow and sighing will flee away. —Isaiah 51:11 (NIV)

11
SATURDAY

All God's gifts are right in front of you as you wait expectantly for our Master Jesus to arrive on the scene for the Finale. —1 Corinthians 1:7 (MSG)

JULY

to pull us through. She never acknowledged defeat under the most trying circumstances. Instead, she used things like a pretty red tablecloth, a couple of red candles, and a bright red apron to create a scene that would never be forgotten by her children.

—*Dorothy Nicholas*

PRAYER REQUESTS

JULY

S	M	T	W	T	F	S
			1	2	3	4
5	6	7	8	9	10	11
12	13	14	15	16	17	18
19	20	21	22	23	24	25
26	27	28	29	30	31	

GUIDEPOSTS DAILY PLANNER

OUR PRAYER
*Lord, empty my mind of all disturbances
so that I can reflect on You.*

---

12 SUNDAY — Give thanks to God—he is good and His love never quits. —1 Chronicles 16:34 (MSG)

---

13 MONDAY — Jesus came and touched them. —Matthew 17:7 (NIV)

---

14 TUESDAY — He must increase, but I must decrease. —John 3:30 (KJV)

WE WERE HIKING in the High Sierras on a crystal-clear midsummer's day. In the high altitude, the sky was deep blue and the color seemed to be intensified in the thin air. My wife, Carol, and I took a trail bordering a fast-rushing stream lined with dusty ferns, rust-colored Indian paintbrush, purple lupine. At the top, we reached a clearing and a glacier-fed lake that was smooth as glass.

"Look," I said to Carol, "you can see the mountains twice."

Sure enough, like a mirror that reflects a face, the lake showed the image of the blue sky, the treeless mountains, the meadow, and the vibrant wildflowers around it. We were reverent, hushed, as though we were in a church. The water was so placid, not a breath of wind rippling its surface, you could see all of nature reflected there.

Staring at the majestic scene, I could almost hear what a minister had once told me about prayer: "Find a place where there are few distractions.

15 WEDNESDAY
There is surely a future hope for you, and your hope will not be cut off.
—Proverbs 23:18 (NIV)

16 THURSDAY
"For I know the plans I have for you," declares the Lord, "plans to prosper you and not to harm you, plans to give you hope and a future." —Jeremiah 29:11 (NIV)

17 FRIDAY
My command is this: Love each other as I have loved you. — John 15:12 (NIV)

18 SATURDAY
Whosoever shall smite thee on thy right cheek, turn to him the other also.
—Matthew 5:39 (KJV)

JULY

Let your body be still and your mind uncluttered with thoughts."

Now I understood why. A mind unruffled, like a lake undisturbed, can more perfectly reflect the glory of God.

—*Rick Hamlin*

PRAYER REQUESTS _____

_____

_____

_____

JULY

S	M	T	W	T	F	S
			1	2	3	4
5	6	7	8	9	10	11
12	13	14	15	16	17	18
19	20	21	22	23	24	25
26	27	28	29	30	31	

OUR PRAYER
Lord, thank You for those who have prayed for us over the years.

---

19 SUNDAY I was found by those who did not seek me; I revealed myself to those who did not ask for me. —Romans 10:20 (NIV)

---

20 MONDAY Every good and perfect gift is from above. —James 1:17 (NIV)

---

21 TUESDAY As for God, his way is perfect: The Lord's word is flawless; he shields all who take refuge in him. —Psalm 18:30 (NIV)

During one of my weekend visits to my 94-year-old father's retirement home in Pennsylvania, Daddy kept gamely trying to stay upright, independent, and awake. The afternoon that I left to drive back to New Jersey, we had a time of prayer as we usually did. Daddy, as always, asked for a safe trip for me, and then added, "Lord, please help me to catch up on my work. I've gotten so far behind."

I chuckled a bit to myself as I drove home, wondering, *What work is he talking about?*

In the next weeks, I discovered what he meant. He was behind in his prayer schedule. For him, prayer was his work. Every day, every week, he had gone through his overflowing loose-leaf notebook filled with letters and prayer requests from friends, missionaries, and missions around the world. As he prayed over every person, every request, he would mark the date.

One reason Daddy had been willing to give up his independence and move to the retirement home was to have more time to pray. But now, he didn't have the energy to go through the book or even to read the new letters that came. Yet as his strength waned and his tongue thickened, he

22
WEDNESDAY

Oh, call your brothers "My People," and your sisters, "Lovingly Accepted."
—Hosea 2:3 (JPS)

23
THURSDAY

. . . that I may know how to sustain the weary one with a word. —Isaiah 50:4 (NASB)

24
FRIDAY

The LORD had said to Abram, "Go from your country, your people and your father's household to the land I will show you." —Genesis 12:1 (NIV)

25
SATURDAY

Some trust in chariots and some in horses, but we trust in the name of the LORD our God. —Psalm 20:7 (NIV)

JULY

would phone friends to find out how they were and what he could pray for as he sat immobilized.

"How much your dad's prayers and interest in us have meant," was the comment that came again and again after his death. "He was a true prayer warrior." What a legacy!

—*Mary Ruth Howes*

PRAYER REQUESTS _____

JULY

S	M	T	W	T	F	S
			1	2	3	4
5	6	7	8	9	10	11
12	13	14	15	16	17	18
19	20	21	22	23	24	25
26	27	28	29	30	31	

GUIDEPOSTS DAILY PLANNER

OUR PRAYER

Dear God, remind me to store up spiritual treasures and not material ones.

26 SUNDAY	Praise the Lord! How good it is to sing praises to our God, for he is gracious, and a song of praise is fitting. —Psalm 147:1 (NRSVUE)	
27 MONDAY	Surely I am with you always, to the very end of the age. —Matthew 28:20 (NIV)	
28 TUESDAY	In the morning, Lord, you hear my voice; in the morning I lay my requests before you and wait expectantly. —Psalm 5:3 (NIV)	

"Why do I get so much junk mail?" I complained to my friend Desila recently. My entire dining room table was covered with mail-order catalogs. Again. An avalanche of colorful pages offered hiking clothes, athletic shoes, kitchen doodads, electronics, even greeting cards and seasonal decorations.

Desila laughed. "It's because you keep ordering out of them!" She was right. Time and again I had found just the item I'd been wanting and placed an order.

After Desila left, I began to paw my way through the mess, tossing out some catalogs, saving others. That's when I noticed it. Buried beneath the barrage of solicitations was my Bible.

Embarrassed, I pulled it out and began flipping through its pages. And, suddenly, I realized that the Bible, too, is a "catalog" of sorts. It tells me how to get peace and contentment (Romans 8:6). It encourages me to ask for joy (John 16:24). It even lets me order laughter (Job 8:21)!

JULY / AUGUST 2026

29
WEDNESDAY

All the days ordained for me were written in your book before one of them came to be. —Psalm 139:16 (NIV)

30
THURSDAY

Jesus answered, "Everyone who drinks this water will be thirsty again, but whoever drinks the water I give them will never thirst." —John 4:13–14 (NIV)

31
FRIDAY

A person finds joy in giving an apt reply—and how good is a timely word! —Proverbs 15:23 (NIV)

AUGUST 1
SATURDAY

Those who know your name trust in you, for you, Lord, have never forsaken those who seek you. —Psalm 9:10 (NIV)

So I've decided to keep the Bible on top of my catalogs. It will remind me that it's not the mail that delivers the things that bring true enjoyment. It's God! And He always gets the order right.

—*Mary Lou Carney*

PRAYER REQUESTS _____

JULY

S	M	T	W	T	F	S
			1	2	3	4
5	6	7	8	9	10	11
12	13	14	15	16	17	18
19	20	21	22	23	24	25
26	27	28	29	30	31	

GUIDEPOSTS DAILY PLANNER

Let us run with perseverance the race marked out for us, fixing our eyes on Jesus, the pioneer and perfecter of faith. —HEBREWS 12:1–2 (NIV)

LIVING A NEW LIFE
Journey Up the Mountain

For weeks I dreaded the approach of my forty-ninth birthday—the beginning of my fiftieth year, surely an apex of my life. I decided to do something symbolic.

"I want to climb a tall mountain," I announced to my family, gazing out our living room window at the front range of the Rockies. I pictured myself sitting atop a high peak, feeling close to God and talking to Him about the prospect of turning 50.

The morning of my birthday, we started up the mountain—two almost-adult children, the dog, and I. We stopped frequently, enjoying the wildflowers and the beautiful vistas. It was nearly noon when we finally pulled ourselves up on the peak. Just then, a blast of wind hit our faces and dark clouds swirled overhead—a dangerous afternoon lightning storm. With a quick glance at the view, we made a hasty retreat.

We got home about dusk, and I went to the window to look at my birthday mountain. But now I saw it in a whole new way—not just as a high peak, but as an entire mountain. I realized I'd made way too much of entering my fiftieth year, because a single apex is not the whole story. What matters most is the step-by-step journey on both sides, which is filled with God's good gifts, like brilliant wildflowers and cool mountain meadows.

—*Carol Kuykendall*

A PRAYER FOR AUGUST

Thanks to You, O God,
that I have risen today,
to the rising of life itself;
may it be to Your own glory,
O God of every gift,
and to the glory
of my soul likewise.

ADAPTED FROM THE CARMINA GADELICA (1891)

AUGUST 2026

AUGUST 2026

SUNDAY	MONDAY	TUESDAY	WEDNESDAY	THURSDAY	FRIDAY	SATURDAY
						1
2	3	4	5	6	7	8
9	10	11	12	13	14	15
16	17	18	19	20	21	22
23 / 30	24 / 31	25	26	27	28	29

NOTES

JULY

S	M	T	W	T	F	S
			1	2	3	4
5	6	7	8	9	10	11
12	13	14	15	16	17	18
19	20	21	22	23	24	25
26	27	28	29	30	31	

SEPTEMBER

S	M	T	W	T	F	S
		1	2	3	4	5
6	7	8	9	10	11	12
13	14	15	16	17	18	19
20	21	22	23	24	25	26
27	28	29	30			

GUIDEPOSTS DAILY PLANNER

OUR PRAYER
Heavenly Father, help us to do our very best on all our projects.

---

2 SUNDAY

Your word is a lamp for my feet, a light on my path. — Psalm 119:105 (NIV)

---

3 MONDAY

Let your ear be attentive and your eyes open to hear the prayer your servant is praying before you day and night. —Nehemiah 1:6 (NIV)

---

4 TUESDAY

How wonderful and pleasant it is when brothers live together in harmony! —Psalm 133:1 (NLT)

"What's troubling you, Harry?" I asked, awakened by my husband's restlessness.

"I'm worrying about the hole we excavated for the foundation today. I think we put too much gravel in there—it's going to make the house too high out of the ground. I got distracted by the work and didn't pay enough attention to the plans."

For months, we had carefully considered the placement of the house on the sloping site. We had already moved it up or down by a foot or two several times—but always on paper. This time was for real.

Yesterday, before the excavating equipment arrived on the scene, we stood on the site and prayed for our house. "Lord, we want this to be Your house. A place of beauty and peace, a place that will welcome others and will nurture us. Help us to be good stewards of what You have given us."

The next morning, we went out to look it over. We measured and marked and debated, and when the contractor arrived we discussed it with him. Over the next few days, as work progressed, it became evident that the higher floor would actually give us a much better view, plus a more usable, walk-out basement instead of a windowless storage area.

5
WEDNESDAY

Forget about deciding what's right for each other. Here's what you need to be concerned about: that you don't get in the way of someone else . . . —Romans 14:13–14 (MSG)

6
THURSDAY

The LORD will guide you always; he . . . will strengthen your frame. —Isaiah 58:11 (NIV)

7
FRIDAY

Therefore, as God's chosen people, holy and dearly loved, clothe yourselves with . . . kindness. —Colossians 3:12 (NIV)

8
SATURDAY

Blessed are they that mourn: for they shall be comforted. —Matthew 5:4 (KJV)

We still find ourselves worrying about things we can't control. But now we have an agreement: Whenever we catch ourselves worrying, our automatic response is, "Whose house is this anyway?"

—*Mary Jane Clark*

PRAYER REQUESTS _____

_____

_____

AUGUST

S	M	T	W	T	F	S
						1
2	3	4	5	6	7	8
9	10	11	12	13	14	15
16	17	18	19	20	21	22
23/30	24/31	25	26	27	28	29

GUIDEPOSTS DAILY PLANNER

OUR PRAYER
Dear Father God, I put my trust in You to meet me at my point of fear.

9 SUNDAY

I will instruct you and teach you in the way you should go; I will counsel you with my loving eye on you. —Psalm 32:8 (NIV)

10 MONDAY

When Jesus heard this, he said to them, "Those who are well have no need of a physician, but those who are sick; I have come to call not the righteous but sinners." —Mark 2:17 (NRSVCE)

11 TUESDAY

Jesus Christ is the same yesterday and today and forever. —Hebrews 13:8 (NIV)

For weeks I'd been putting off a phone call to schedule some rather unpleasant intestinal tests. I dreaded both the tests and the possible results. I'd tell myself, *I'll do it today*, but when evening came, the call was still unmade. Then at a picnic in the park one day, God met me at my point of fear.

Seated on our picnic blanket, my husband John and I watched the family next to us. The children, four of them, spun themselves about, then took turns falling backward into their father's arms. One little tot was apprehensive. He giggled and laughed as his brothers spun him, but he was too afraid to let himself fall. We watched as the whole family urged the little fellow on. When finally he got up the gumption to trust his dad and fell into his arms, we all clapped our hands and yelled, "Yeah!" Suddenly, there was no stopping him—he did it again and again until the other children insisted on their turns.

"Dear Lord," I prayed that night, "I'm afraid to take these tests, but I will put my trust in Your everlasting arms. I know You will catch me and set me on my feet again." I could almost hear God's voice shouting, "Yeah!"

12 WEDNESDAY
I have calmed and quieted my soul, like a weaned child with its mother; my soul is like the weaned child that is with me. —Psalm 131:2 (NRSVUE)

13 THURSDAY
In quietness and confidence shall be your strength. —Isaiah 30:15 (NKJV)

14 FRIDAY
If anyone serves, they should do so with the strength God provides. —1 Peter 4:11 (NIV)

15 SATURDAY
Again I say to you, if two of you agree on earth about anything they ask, it will be done for them by my Father in heaven. —Matthew 18:19 (ESV)

AUGUST

The next morning I made the appointment, and a few days later I took the tests. They were not easy, but I was not afraid as I took the plunge. My Father's arms were there. And the results of the tests showed no problems.

—*Fay Angus*

PRAYER REQUESTS _____

AUGUST

S	M	T	W	T	F	S
						1
2	3	4	5	6	7	8
9	10	11	12	13	14	15
16	17	18	19	20	21	22
23/30	24/31	25	26	27	28	29

GUIDEPOSTS DAILY PLANNER

OUR PRAYER
Lord, sometimes bigger isn't better.
Help me to live a manageable life.

---

16 SUNDAY

But I trust in you, Lord; I say, "You are my God." My times are in your hands. —Psalm 31:14–15 (NIV)

---

17 MONDAY

So in Christ we, though many, form one body, and each member belongs to all the others. We have different gifts, according to the grace given to each of us. —Romans 12:5–6 (NIV)

---

18 TUESDAY

Hope deferred makes the heart sick, but a longing fulfilled is a tree of life. —Proverbs 13:12 (NIV)

An old teacher friend of mine, Norval Campbell, once advised me, "Don't make your garden so large that you can't tend it." I didn't understand his advice at the time, but I do now—after our area experienced a major flood.

The heavy rains that started in the spring and never let up discouraged me from having my usual large garden out behind the college where I teach. Instead, I just set out a few things around the house: four tomato plants, a dozen okra plants, a few flowers and some asparagus.

I was amazed to discover that this little planting gave me more pleasure than my large garden, and plenty of produce. The reason? The small garden was more manageable. The bigger garden was always ahead of me with weeds and bugs and the need for cultivation. But four tomato plants? I could weed, water, and fertilize them, stake them, and check them for worms in only a few minutes a week. And those four produced more tomatoes

19
WEDNESDAY

You keep track of all my sorrows. You have collected all my tears in your bottle. You have recorded each one in your book. —Psalm 56:8 (NLT)

20
THURSDAY

A joyful heart is good medicine, but a crushed spirit dries up the bones. —Proverbs 17:22 (ESV)

21
FRIDAY

Cast your burden on the Lord, and he will sustain you; he will never permit the righteous to be moved. —Psalm 55:22 (ESV)

22
SATURDAY

Don't be anxious about tomorrow. God will take care of your tomorrow, too. Live one day at a time. —Matthew 6:34 (TLB)

---

than the fifteen plants I had last year, and I had enough okra to feed the neighbors, too.

Overextending is an easy mistake to make. Next time I'm tempted to do too much, I'll remember my garden.

—*Daniel Schantz*

PRAYER REQUESTS _____

AUGUST

S	M	T	W	T	F	S
						1
2	3	4	5	6	7	8
9	10	11	12	13	14	15
16	17	18	19	20	21	22
23/30	24/31	25	26	27	28	29

GUIDEPOSTS DAILY PLANNER

OUR PRAYER
Father, thank You for answering my doubts as well as my prayers.

---

23 SUNDAY

How abundant are the good things that you have stored up for those who fear you, that you bestow in the sight of all, on those who take refuge in you. —Psalm 31:19 (NIV)

---

24 MONDAY

Each day is God's gift. . . .Whatever turns up, grab it and do it. And heartily! —Ecclesiastes 9:8–9 (MSG)

---

25 TUESDAY

Be joyful. Grow to maturity. Encourage each other. Live in harmony and peace. Then the God of love and peace will be with you. —2 Corinthians 13:11 (NLT)

A FEW YEARS AGO, on a trip to Scotland, I took a bus to Loch Ness. On the way, I got to talking to the driver, who explained how to catch the return bus. "I'm sorry I cannot be your driver then," he said with a grin. "We trade off. But the chap who'll take you back is a fine bloke indeed."

Two minutes after disembarking, I discovered I'd left my camera on the bus! And my American immigrant card—which I needed to return to the U.S.—was in the case. "Oh, God," I prayed, "I need to get my camera back!" But even as I prayed, I doubted. The chances of getting it back were almost nil.

When I called the station back in Inverness, I was told that that particular bus was starting its return trip and would be coming past the very phone booth I was calling from in about two minutes. I'd no sooner hung up than the bus rumbled to a stop five yards away. I couldn't believe it, but it was my bus driver who opened the doors and held out my camera!

"I thought you were trading buses," I said, running to thank him.

"Aye! But I saw your camera, and I knew your

26 WEDNESDAY
Create in me a clean heart, God, and renew a steadfast spirit within me.
—Psalm 51:10 (NASB)

27 THURSDAY
I am not worthy of all the unfailing love and faithfulness you have shown to me.
—Genesis 32:10 (NLT)

28 FRIDAY
"The Lord bless you and keep you; the Lord make his face shine on you and be gracious to you." —Numbers 6:24–25 (NIV)

29 SATURDAY
May your fountain be blessed, and may you rejoice in the wife of your youth.
—Proverbs 5:18 (NIV)

---

heart would be broken if I didn't take care of you and bring it back. So I traded to keep my own bus."

What an answer for my doubts! 'Tis plain I have a fine Bloke indeed who watches out for me. As He does for us all.

—*Brenda Wilbee*

PRAYER REQUESTS _____

AUGUST

S	M	T	W	T	F	S
						1
2	3	4	5	6	7	8
9	10	11	12	13	14	15
16	17	18	19	20	21	22
23/30	24/31	25	26	27	28	29

GUIDEPOSTS DAILY PLANNER

For I know the thoughts that I think toward you, says the LORD, *thoughts of peace and not of evil, to give you a future and a hope.* —JEREMIAH 29:11 (NKJV)

A PRAYER FOR SEPTEMBER

Lord, thank You for this
September morning.
The crisp coolness
in the breeze reminds me
that this is a new season. . . .
Thank You, Father,
that the excitement
and anticipation
of that fresh new beginning
is born again in my soul
on a September morning.

CAROL KUYKENDALL

LIVING A NEW LIFE
Follow the Signs

I was grappling with the decision to move to the Canadian Rockies. God—and my instincts—seem to say, "Go!" The schools were good, the air was dry and much better for my health, and the job situation was fruitful. But I still had a lot of fears. So as a test, my children and I went to the Rockies for a vacation.

One day my daughter, Heather, and I dropped the boys off at the ski slopes and headed east for the prairies. On the way back, Heather drove. "Let's take the back roads," she suggested.

As we wound through the foothills, she saw a sign: "Buffalo Paddock." Next thing I knew she had veered off the road, bumping and flying on narrow dirt tracks until we came to a screeching halt.

There they were! A whole herd of buffalo, milling about just below a cliff. Heather was quite pleased with herself. I was, too. Such a marvelous sense of adventure!

Remembering that afternoon, I can see my way a bit more clearly now. I've wanted God to guide me, but I've been ignoring the signs that point to adventure, afraid to leave the main road. Now, like Heather, I'm going to search for something wonderful, even if it means a rough and bumpy road. I'm trusting God to guide me.

—*Brenda Wilbee*

SEPTEMBER 2026

SUNDAY	MONDAY	TUESDAY	WEDNESDAY	THURSDAY	FRIDAY	SATURDAY
		1	2	3	4	5
6	7 LABOR DAY	8	9	10	11 ROSH HASHANAH BEGINS AT SUNDOWN	12
13	14	15	16	17 CITIZENSHIP DAY	18	19
20 YOM KIPPUR BEGINS AT SUNDOWN	21	22 FALL BEGINS	23	24	25	26
27	28	29	30			

NOTES

AUGUST

S	M	T	W	T	F	S
						1
2	3	4	5	6	7	8
9	10	11	12	13	14	15
16	17	18	19	20	21	22
23/30	24/31	25	26	27	28	29

OCTOBER

S	M	T	W	T	F	S
				1	2	3
4	5	6	7	8	9	10
11	12	13	14	15	16	17
18	19	20	21	22	23	24
25	26	27	28	29	30	31

GUIDEPOSTS DAILY PLANNER

OUR PRAYER
Lord, thank You for giving us what it takes to challenge life's trails.

30 SUNDAY

As they rode along, they came to some water, and the eunuch said, "Look! There's some water! Why can't I be baptized?" He ordered the carriage to stop, and they went down into the water, and Philip baptized him. —Acts 8:36–38 (NLT)

31 MONDAY

You shall anoint for Me the one I point out to you. —1 Samuel 16:3 (JPS)

SEPTEMBER 1 TUESDAY

A good word maketh [the heart] glad. —Proverbs 12:25 (KJV)

OUR KIDS HAD DONE it, and they raved about the experience. True, they were teenagers and we were "fortysomething"—but certainly we could manage a 38-mile, 4-day backpack trip. Or so my husband, Terry, and I thought when we joined friends Dave and Anita at the start of Alaska's Resurrection Trail last August.

After the first 2 miles, our "fortysomething" body parts began sending out alarming signals. Anita's old, too-tight boots cramped her toes so badly she barely hobbled to our first camp. By the second day my shoulders were screaming from carrying a 40-pound pack. Dave cut up part of his foam sleeping pad to use as extra cushioning under my shoulder straps, and then more of it to cushion his agonized feet.

We attained Resurrection Summit on the third day, and we laughed ourselves senseless over another hiker's entry in the trail log book: "Came in pain, slept in pain, left in pain!"

What's hard to figure is that we were actually sorry when the hike was over. We had traversed some fantastic country, the memory of which was ours to keep. We'd shared our campfire with a fellow traveler and talked about how Jesus walks

2
WEDNESDAY

We were gentle among you, like a nursing mother taking care of her own children. —1 Thessalonians 2:7 (ESV)

3
THURSDAY

Remember the Sabbath day by keeping it holy. —Exodus 20:8 (NIV)

4
FRIDAY

As iron sharpens iron, so one person sharpens another. —Proverbs 27:17 (NIV)

5
SATURDAY

Give, and it will be given to you. Good measure, pressed down, shaken together, running over, will be put into your lap. For with the measure you use it will be measured back to you. —Luke 6:38 (ESV)

---

with us along our personal trails. And we discovered that the things that got us up the Resurrection Trail were the same things that have brought us this far along in life. I think we "fortysomethings" are going to keep on making our way just fine.

—*Carol Knapp*

PRAYER REQUESTS _____

SEPTEMBER

S	M	T	W	T	F	S
		1	2	3	4	5
6	7	8	9	10	11	12
13	14	15	16	17	18	19
20	21	22	23	24	25	26
27	28	29	30			

GUIDEPOSTS DAILY PLANNER

OUR PRAYER
Lord, help me to remember the investment You have made in each of us, so that I won't forget to reinvest in others.

---

6 SUNDAY

To every thing there is a season, and a time to every purpose under the heaven. —Ecclesiastes 3:1 (KJV)

---

7 MONDAY — LABOR DAY

The LORD God, even my God, will be with thee; he will not fail thee, nor forsake thee, until thou hast finished all the work for the service of the house of the LORD. —1 Chronicles 28:20 (KJV)

---

8 TUESDAY

The LORD bless you and keep you; the LORD make his face shine on you and be gracious to you; the LORD turn his face toward you and give you peace. —Numbers 6:24–26 (NIV)

At breakfast, I pore over my *Wall Street Journal*. "How are your stocks today, Brock?" my mother asks.

"Great! Just think, Mom, if I work hard and invest wisely, in about 10 years my portfolio will be worth a fortune."

Stocks and bonds, the highs and lows of the market have been a passion of mine since high school. My mom has heard all of this before. "Mmm" is her response as she wipes the crumbs from the counter.

Later that day, Mom, my sister, Keri, and I are at the mall. All of a sudden, a boy who has to be 6 feet 6 inches walks up to us. "Hello, Mrs. Kidd!" the boy grins.

"Hi, Bo!" my mom replies. She asks about his mother, his math grades, and basketball camp. Before he leaves us, Bo bends over and hugs Mom, practically lifting her off the ground.

"Mom, who was that?" I had never seen the boy before and was a little confused.

My mother was answering, "Oh, just a friend..." when Keri interrupted, explaining that Mom had found out that Bo didn't have the money to go to camp last summer, so she and Dad paid.

My parents will never get ahead financially, I thought. "Mom, how could you afford the extra expense?"

SEPTEMBER 2026

9 WEDNESDAY

Pray without ceasing. —1 Thessalonians 5:17 (NASB)

10 THURSDAY

Be patient like those farmers and don't give up. —James 5:8 (CEV)

11 FRIDAY
ROSH HASHANAH BEGINS AT SUNDOWN

But God demonstrates his own love for us in this: while we were still sinners, Christ died for us. —Romans 5:8 (NIV)

12 SATURDAY

To get wisdom is to love oneself; to keep understanding is to prosper. —Proverbs 19:8 (NRSVUE)

Mom smiled her wonderful smile and said, "I have my own portfolio. It's just that your dad and I sort of lean toward people investments."

I had to laugh at myself then. Mom had just handed me the investment tip of a lifetime.

—*Brock Kidd*

PRAYER REQUESTS _____

SEPTEMBER

S	M	T	W	T	F	S
		1	2	3	4	5
6	7	8	9	10	11	12
13	14	15	16	17	18	19
20	21	22	23	24	25	26
27	28	29	30			

GUIDEPOSTS DAILY PLANNER

OUR PRAYER

Father in heaven, remind me to walk in someone else's shoes before I cast the first stones of my anger.

---

13 SUNDAY

The sheep hear his voice. He calls his own sheep by name and leads them out. —John 10:3 (NRSVUE)

---

14 MONDAY

So I came out to meet you; I looked for you and have found you! —Proverbs 7:15 (NIV)

---

15 TUESDAY

. . . and with your feet fitted with the readiness that comes from the gospel of peace. —Ephesians 6:15 (NIV)

ONE HOT MORNING, I was sitting on the deck reading the newspaper when I heard this loud, irritating whirring noise. I turned the page, expecting the noise to stop eventually, but it didn't.

Finally I stood up from my chair and stepped around the corner of the house. I looked up, and there it was—an attic fan in my neighbor's house making a terrible racket. My neighbor had installed it the day before.

For the next few days, I complained to my wife about the noise. Finally, I walked over to my neighbor's house and pressed the doorbell. My defense was prepared. My anger was controlled. I was going to ask him to disconnect the fan.

"Hi, Chris," my neighbor warmly greeted me. "Come on in."

"How are you, Jerry?" I asked as we shook hands.

"Well, better," he said. "We've had a bit of a scare the last few weeks. My daughter Anna developed a terrible breathing problem. The doctor suggested fresh air in the house, not air conditioning, so I installed an attic fan. Now she finally sleeps at night again, so all is OK."

Jerry looked at me. I looked at him. Then he

SEPTEMBER 2026

16
WEDNESDAY

Understand this, my dear brothers and sisters: You must all be quick to listen, slow to speak, and slow to get angry. —James 1:19 (NLT)

17
THURSDAY

CITIZENSHIP DAY

A word fitly spoken is like apples of gold in pictures of silver. —Proverbs 25:11 (KJV)

18
FRIDAY

Now faith is confidence in what we hope for and assurance about what we do not see. —Hebrews 11:1 (NIV)

19
SATURDAY

For where your treasure is, there your heart will be also. —Matthew 6:21 (ESV)

---

asked, "What's new with you?"

"Well," I said, "I . . . ah . . . was wondering if I could borrow your hedge clippers."

When I returned to my house, I sat on my deck for the rest of the afternoon. The noisy fan has never bothered me since.

—*Christopher de Vinck*

PRAYER REQUESTS _____

_____

_____

SEPTEMBER

S	M	T	W	T	F	S
		1	2	3	4	5
6	7	8	9	10	11	12
13	14	15	16	17	18	19
20	21	22	23	24	25	26
27	28	29	30			

GUIDEPOSTS DAILY PLANNER

OUR PRAYER
Dear Lord, please help me remember to bestow the kisses today that I want loved ones to remember tomorrow.

---

20 SUNDAY
YOM KIPPUR BEGINS AT SUNDOWN

"Blessed are the merciful, for they will receive mercy." —Matthew 5:7 (NRSVCE)

---

21 MONDAY

I rejoiced with those who said to me, "Let us go to the house of the Lord." —Psalm 122:1 (NIV)

---

22 TUESDAY
FALL BEGINS

For who is God save the Lord? or who is a rock save our God? —Psalm 18:31 (KJV)

Tonight tragedy hit home when I found out from my boyfriend's little brother, Geoff, that a 14-year-old boy who went to camp with Geoff had committed suicide.

I raced into my parents' bedroom to tell them the terrible news as soon as I got home. My mother was getting ready for bed, and when I told her what had happened, she sighed and lay down in bed. "Oh, God," she said, "how awful. How simply awful."

"Imagine," I said, and swallowed hard. "He was only 14 years old." Geoff was almost 14, and my twin sisters were 15. The thought of one of them taking his or her own life was unbearable.

"His poor family," my mother added sadly. "Please pray for that boy tonight, Jennifer."

"I will, Mom," I promised, and then bent down to kiss her forehead.

"To what do I owe the pleasure?" my mother mumbled drowsily.

"Since when do I need a reason to kiss my own mother?" I joked, but she had already drifted off, so I quietly left the room.

23
WEDNESDAY

Dearly loved friends, don't always believe everything you hear just because someone says it is a message from God: test it first to see if it really is. —1 John 4:1 (TLB)

24
THURSDAY

I urge, then, first of all, that petitions, prayers, intercession and thanksgiving be made for all people. —1 Timothy 2:1 (NIV)

25
FRIDAY

Just as a body, though one, has many parts, but all its many parts form one body, so it is with Christ. —1 Corinthians 12:12 (NIV)

26
SATURDAY

My God will meet all your needs according to the riches of his glory in Christ Jesus. —Philippians 4:19 (NIV)

There's another mother in this world tonight who won't be receiving kisses from her child, I thought to myself as I walked into my room. And as I knelt beside my bed to pray for all the kisses lost in the world today, I also thanked God for all the kisses I had yet to give.

—*Jennifer Thomas*

PRAYER REQUESTS _____

SEPTEMBER

S	M	T	W	T	F	S
		1	2	3	4	5
6	7	8	9	10	11	12
13	14	15	16	17	18	19
20	21	22	23	24	25	26
27	28	29	30			

GUIDEPOSTS DAILY PLANNER

OUR PRAYER
Lord, help me to look beyond my fears to Your good world.

---

27 SUNDAY

Consider it pure joy, my brothers and sisters, whenever you face trials of many kinds, because you know that the testing of your faith produces perseverance. —James 1:2–3 (NIV)

---

28 MONDAY

Our citizenship is in heaven, and from it we await a Savior, the Lord Jesus Christ, who will transform our lowly body to be like his glorious body. —Philippians 3:20–21 (ESV)

---

29 TUESDAY

Woe to the world because of the things that cause people to stumble! Such things must come, but woe to the person through whom they come! —Matthew 18:7 (NIV)

"Forewarned is forearmed," my husband said after watching a TV program on crimes in schools. He handed me a tiny black disk that fit in the palm of a hand. "If a student tries to attack you, press this little button." A horrible sound pierced my eardrums, then suddenly ceased.

The first day I carried it in my pocket, the small alarm felt as heavy as a battering ram. Instead of my usual confident stride, I walked slowly, hesitantly throughout the day. Everything and everyone on campus looked eerie, suspicious, sinister.

Then, coming through a secluded grove of trees on my way to my car, I spied a shadowy, menacing figure sprinting toward me. My eyes traced with alarm the stranger's hulking frame, the baseball cap turned backward, the gold earring sparkling in one ear, the hooded eyes.

I groped for the alarm. Yet as I found the button, the stranger's eyes opened wide, a grin spread from ear to ear, and a hand waved wildly in greeting. It was Pete, a favorite student. As he came into a patch of sunlight, the world suddenly shifted into focus and I saw him clearly, untainted by my unwarranted fears. Just Pete, a friendly young man in

30
WEDNESDAY

For if either of them falls, the one will lift up his companion. —Ecclesiastes 4:10 (NASB)

OCTOBER 1
THURSDAY

Your paths drip with fatness. —Psalm 65:11 (NASB)

2
FRIDAY

The Lord makes firm the steps of the one who delights in him. —Psalm 37:23 (NIV)

3
SATURDAY

Hold on to what is good. —1 Thessalonians 5:21 (NIV)

---

a friendly place where good things abounded.

I still carry the black disk. But I don't let it limit my perspective or make me see friends as enemies. More importantly, I go armed with the courage that faith bestows.

—*Linda Ching Sledge*

PRAYER REQUESTS _____

SEPTEMBER

S	M	T	W	T	F	S
		1	2	3	4	5
6	7	8	9	10	11	12
13	14	15	16	17	18	19
20	21	22	23	24	25	26
27	28	29	30			

GUIDEPOSTS DAILY PLANNER

I am reminded of your sincere faith, a faith that dwelt first in your grandmother. —2 TIMOTHY 1:5 (RSV)

A PRAYER FOR OCTOBER

Teach me, O Spirit of God,
the silent language which says all things.
Teach my soul to remain silent
in Your presence.
That I may adore You in the depths
  of my being
and await all things from You,
asking nothing of You
but the accomplishment of Your will.

JOHN NICHOLAS GROU (1731–1803)

LIVING A NEW LIFE
Returning Good for Evil

Outside my grandparents' home one day, a neighbor's child suddenly announced, "I don't like you."

Well, I ran crying to Grandma, who wrapped her arms around me and kissed me. "Let's see if a cookie will help," she said. Grandma was right. A cookie, plus a glass of cold milk, did help. But soon anger replaced the tears.

"I'm going back out there and tell that Emily I don't like her either!" I announced.

"Tell you what," Grandma answered. "Why don't you ask her to come inside and have some cookies too? Remember, the Bible says we should return good for evil." I glowered in skepticism, but finally gave in.

Grandma was right again. The promise of another cookie did it. Soon Emily and I were cutting out paper dolls in the front room, then playing jacks on the sidewalk. That was the beginning of our being best friends.

Now I am a grandmother, nearly 70 years later, and not much has changed. I still believe that returning good for evil is the best way to treat others. I'm thankful that I learned that early in life from my dear grandmother. It is the seed I want to plant in the tender hearts of my growing grandchildren.

—Isabel Wolseley

OCTOBER 2026

SUNDAY	MONDAY	TUESDAY	WEDNESDAY	THURSDAY	FRIDAY	SATURDAY
				1	2	3
4 WORLD COMMUNION SUNDAY	5	6	7	8	9	10
11	12	13	14	15	16	17
18	19	20	21	22	23	24 UNITED NATIONS DAY
25	26	27	28	29	30	31 HALLOWEEN

NOTES

SEPTEMBER

S	M	T	W	T	F	S
		1	2	3	4	5
6	7	8	9	10	11	12
13	14	15	16	17	18	19
20	21	22	23	24	25	26
27	28	29	30			

NOVEMBER

S	M	T	W	T	F	S
1	2	3	4	5	6	7
8	9	10	11	12	13	14
15	16	17	18	19	20	21
22	23	24	25	26	27	28
29	30					

GUIDEPOSTS DAILY PLANNER

OUR PRAYER

Lord God, open my eyes to wonder more often so that I can see the everyday as You do.

---

4 / SUNDAY / WORLD COMMUNION DAY

I will give them an undivided heart and put a new spirit in them. —Ezekiel 11:19 (NIV)

---

5 / MONDAY

Trust in the Lord with all your heart and lean not on your own understanding. —Proverbs 3:5 (NIV)

---

6 / TUESDAY

He has made everything beautiful in its time. He has also set eternity in the human heart. —Ecclesiastes 3:11 (NIV)

One early, ordinary fall morning, I sleepily dragged myself to the deck to shake the kitchen rug. Yuck! A cloud of dog hairs and dirt dissolved into my backyard. I turned to go inside, but something out there caught the corner of my eye. On the edge of our pond was a dignified guest, a great heron, standing stock-still on one skinny leg, long sharp beak in profile, as if waiting for its portrait to be finished. Leaning on the railing, I watched it, thrilled at this out-of-the-ordinary, exotic creature visiting my common turf.

Finally, it turned its long beak my way, a spray of head feathers nodding, and gave me a haughty look that said, "Toodle-loo." Spreading enormous wings, it soared over the treetops and on to whatever place it goes for the winter. "Wait!" I wanted to shout. "Stay and be my guest. Live here, so I can thrill to your sight every morning."

I could almost hear it call across the sharp, clean breeze, "How long before I, too, become ordinary?" As I looked around at the wild ducks paddling sparkling wakes in a clear, oval pond, the cloudless sapphire sky spread like a tent pegged

7
WEDNESDAY

I lie down and sleep, and all night long the LORD protects me. I am not afraid of the thousands of enemies who surround me on every side. —Psalm 3:5–6 (GNT)

8
THURSDAY

The nations will see your vindication, and all kings your glory; you will be called by a new name that the mouth of the LORD will bestow. —Isaiah 62:2 (NIV)

9
FRIDAY

You will be my witnesses. —Acts 1:8 (ESV)

10
SATURDAY

Do everything in love. —1 Corinthians 16:14 (NIV)

---

with rich crimson trees, the green carpeted field fringed in morning shadows, the calico cat expertly stalking the fence line, I knew the great heron had been sent to tell me, "Wake up and see your astonishing backyard!"

—*Shari Smyth*

PRAYER REQUESTS _____

OCTOBER

S	M	T	W	T	F	S
				1	2	3
4	5	6	7	8	9	10
11	12	13	14	15	16	17
18	19	20	21	22	23	24
25	26	27	28	29	30	31

GUIDEPOSTS DAILY PLANNER

OUR PRAYER
Lord, I believe. Help my unbelief.

11 SUNDAY — The purpose in a man's heart is like deep water, but a man of understanding will draw it out. —Proverbs 20:5 (ESV)

12 MONDAY — I have learned, in whatever state I am, to be content. —Philippians 4:11 (RSV)

13 TUESDAY — The Spirit himself testifies with our spirit that we are God's children. —Romans 8:16 (NIV)

LORD, I BELIEVE; *help Thou mine unbelief.* After my husband's father, John David Kidd, died, we found references to these words time after time in his papers and books.

How strange. Here I was with an indelible memory of a peaceful man who sat every evening of his life in a worn chair, haloed by an old floor lamp, reading his Bible. He seemed so steadfast. He had studied the book from cover to cover until the entire volume was soft and pliable. And yet penciled here and there, the same words kept coming up: "Lord, I believe. Help my unbelief."

It's been more than 4 years since Dad Kidd died. In those years, it would be impossible to count the number of times those words have come to comfort me. How can I ever have Keri's tuition saved by August? "Lord, I believe. Help my unbelief," I whisper. I don't think I can handle all of the things I have to do . . . the house, the job, the church work. "Lord, I believe. Help my unbelief," I whisper again.

There's something so hopeful in knowing that a man as faithful as Dad Kidd struggled, as I struggle, to maintain what seemed to be an imperishable brand

14
WEDNESDAY

She watches over the affairs of her household and does not eat the bread of idleness. —Proverbs 31:27 (NIV)

15
THURSDAY

Seek ye first the kingdom of God, and his righteousness; and all these things shall be added unto you. —Matthew 6:33 (KJV)

16
FRIDAY

Do not let your hearts be troubled and do not be afraid. —John 14:27 (NIV)

17
SATURDAY

Moses was one hundred twenty years old when he died; his sight was unimpaired, and his vigor had not abated. —Deuteronomy 34:7 (NRSVUE)

---

of faith. He, too, needed a touchstone to strengthen his believing. Like Dad Kidd, I want to believe that God will carry me over the rough spots and set me down in cool, sweet places of rest and happiness. And so I pray, as he did, "Lord, I believe...."

—*Pam Kidd*

OCTOBER

S	M	T	W	T	F	S
					1	2	3
4	5	6	7	8	9	10
11	12	13	14	15	16	17
18	19	20	21	22	23	24
25	26	27	28	29	30	31

PRAYER REQUESTS _____

_____

_____

_____

OCTOBER

GUIDEPOSTS DAILY PLANNER

OUR PRAYER
Lord, hear my prayers, and bless the people whose lives I encounter.

18 SUNDAY — May your blessing be on your people. —Psalm 3:8 (NIV)

19 MONDAY — A gentle answer turns away wrath, but harsh words cause quarrels. —Proverbs 15:1 (TLB)

20 TUESDAY — This is the genealogy of Jesus the Messiah the son of David, the son of Abraham. —Matthew 1:1 (NIV)

I USED TO WORK part-time as a photo stylist for several home decorating publications. My job took me into a lot of different homes, where I arranged flowers and food and help make a room look "picture perfect" for the camera's eye.

One morning, I was working alone in a guest bedroom, I began to think about the guests who would spend a night in that cozy room. I found myself praying for their comfort and well-being.

And so it was that I began my secret practice of whispering a prayer in every room at a photo shoot. At Thanksgiving time, as I helped the photographer move a heavy dining room table, I asked God to bless those who would gather there. Later, fluffing pillows in a toddler's bedroom, I prayed for a young life devoted to serving the Lord. Often, though, I wondered if my prayers did any good.

Then one summer evening, I received a long-distance phone call from a homeowner. "You don't really know my daughter Amy," the lady said, "but I noticed you smiling at her picture the day you photographed our home. I wanted to tell you, her cancer's in remission."

21
WEDNESDAY

When I am afraid, I put my trust in You. —Psalm 56:3 (NIV)

22
THURSDAY

The eyes of the LORD are on the righteous, and his ears are attentive to their cry. —Psalm 34:15 (NIV)

23
FRIDAY

You are the God who works wonders; you have made known your might among the peoples. —Psalm 77:14 (ESV)

24
SATURDAY

UNITED NATIONS DAY

Moses' arms soon became so tired he could no longer hold them up. So Aaron and Hur found a stone for him to sit on. Then they stood on each side of Moses, holding up his hands. So his hands held steady until sunset. —Exodus 17:12 (NLT)

That first of many such reports confirmed my decision to make every photo shoot (as well as every visit to a friend or loved one's home) an opportunity for prayer—prayer whispered in secret as I move quietly from room to room.

—*Roberta Messner*

PRAYER REQUESTS _____

OCTOBER

S	M	T	W	T	F	S
				1	2	3
4	5	6	7	8	9	10
11	12	13	14	15	16	17
18	19	20	21	22	23	24
25	26	27	28	29	30	31

OCTOBER

GUIDEPOSTS DAILY PLANNER

OUR PRAYER
*Lord, help me to create prayer reminders
in my heart and in my home.*

---

25 SUNDAY

The soothing tongue is a tree of life. —Proverbs 15:4 (NIV)

---

26 MONDAY

Be strong and of a good courage. —Deuteronomy 31:6 (KJV)

---

27 TUESDAY

Truly I tell you, whatever you did for one of the least of these brothers and sisters of mine, you did for me. —Matthew 25:40 (NIV)

MY PRAYER LIFE needed help. I'd been searching for a way to help me pray more consistently. The one I discovered is so simple, I almost hesitate to share it.

While I was cleaning out my walk-in closet one day, an eight-by-ten photograph of my twin sons fell from a top shelf. Jon and Jeremy were four in the picture, wearing navy sailor suits with short pants and white, starched collars and new, red-buckle shoes. I smiled at the picture I had thought was lost and started to replace it on the shelf when an idea came to me. I taped the picture to the wall, eye-level, in a spot where no clothes hung. Then I bowed my head and prayed for each son. Later, I added pictures of my other children and grandchildren. My husband's picture is there, too—I know some special dreams and visions he has. I've included a picture of a friend who needs a big miracle, as well as pictures of other friends, and things to remind me of some of my dreams. It's become my prayer wall.

My intercession over my collage of prayer requests is sometimes lengthy. Then I sit or kneel

OCTOBER 2026

28
WEDNESDAY

Let him have all your worries and cares, for he is always thinking about you and watching everything that concerns you. —1 Peter 5:7 (TLB)

29
THURSDAY

Praise be to the name of God for ever and ever; wisdom and power are his. —Daniel 2:20 (NIV)

30
FRIDAY

You can't hide behind a religious mask forever; sooner or later the mask will slip and your true face will be known. —Luke 12:2 (MSG)

31
SATURDAY
HALLOWEEN

The path of the righteous is like the morning sun, shining ever brighter till the full light of day. —Proverbs 4:18 (NIV)

---

amid my shoes. Other times I'm grabbing something in a hurry, and a glance at my prayer wall reminds me to pray on the go. But whether my prayer time is long or brief, I sense that in my closet I'm in a snug, secure cocoon of prayer, with no outside interferences.

—*Marion Bond West*

PRAYER REQUESTS _____

OCTOBER

S	M	T	W	T	F	S
				1	2	3
4	5	6	7	8	9	10
11	12	13	14	15	16	17
18	19	20	21	22	23	24
25	26	27	28	29	30	31

GUIDEPOSTS DAILY PLANNER

Continue steadfastly in prayer. —COLOSSIANS 4:2 (RSV)

A PRAYER FOR NOVEMBER

Thanks to You,
my joy and my glory and my confidence,
my God, thanks to You for Your gifts,
preserve them in me,
for so will You preserve me,
and those things You have given me
shall increase and be perfected,
and I myself shall be with You,
because even my existence is Your gift.

ST. AUGUSTINE OF HIPPO (354–430)

LIVING A NEW LIFE
A Way to Help Others

I do not sleep well nowadays. I've been getting up and going out to the living room to sit in my large, comfortable recliner to pray. In the quietness of the night, it's very easy; God seems very near.

One night I found myself saying, "Lord, let me count for something in this world. I'm housebound now, and my active life is over, but isn't there something I can still do to help others?"

The next morning I awoke with the very distinct feeling that I should call an elderly lady I knew who was in very poor health. She was elated and so eager to talk. As I hung up the telephone, I suddenly knew that this was the answer to my prayer the night before. After breakfast, I called another shut-in, and another, and another.

My husband commented, "You do have 'telephonitis' today."

"No," I replied, "it's just that God has shown me an opportunity to make a difference in the lives of others, even after I'd started thinking my days of activity were over."

"Then go for it," he replied.

From that day onward I've continued calling at least six people every day, sometimes an even dozen. It's when I lose count of my calls that I know I can still count for some good in this world.

—Dorothy Nicholas

NOVEMBER 2026

SUNDAY	MONDAY	TUESDAY	WEDNESDAY	THURSDAY	FRIDAY	SATURDAY
1 ALL SAINTS' DAY DAYLIGHT SAVING TIME ENDS	**2** ALL SOUL'S DAY	**3** ELECTION DAY	**4**	**5**	**6**	**7**
8	**9**	**10**	**11** VETERANS DAY	**12**	**13**	**14**
15	**16**	**17**	**18**	**19**	**20**	**21**
22 NATIONAL BIBLE WEEK BEGINS	**23** GUIDEPOSTS THANKSGIVING DAY OF PRAYER	**24**	**25**	**26** THANKSGIVING	**27**	**28**
29 1ST SUNDAY IN ADVENT	**30**					

NOTES

OCTOBER

S	M	T	W	T	F	S
				1	2	3
4	5	6	7	8	9	10
11	12	13	14	15	16	17
18	19	20	21	22	23	24
25	26	27	28	29	30	31

DECEMBER

S	M	T	W	T	F	S
		1	2	3	4	5
6	7	8	9	10	11	12
13	14	15	16	17	18	19
20	21	22	23	24	25	26
27	28	29	30	31		

GUIDEPOSTS DAILY PLANNER

OUR PRAYER
*Dear God, I thank You for Your saints and
the path they have left for us.*

1 SUNDAY
ALL SAINTS' DAY
DAYLIGHT SAVING TIME ENDS

I have called you by name; you are mine. —Isaiah 43:1 (RSV)

2 MONDAY
ALL SOUL'S DAY

The LORD is near to the brokenhearted and saves those who are crushed in spirit. —Psalm 34:18 (NASB)

3 TUESDAY
ELECTION DAY

Still I cling to your laws and obey them. —Psalm 119:83 (TLB)

ONE OF THE THINGS I like best about my small Midwestern hometown is its cemetery, complete with quaint wrought-iron fence and winding gravel driveway. Near that driveway is a small cement bench with these words engraved on its side: *Come Sit with Us.*

When I was a child, I thought it a strange invitation. But as I grew up—and people I cared about died—I often did just that. I would sit on the cool stone bench and look around at the headstones of those I had known: Roger, who died in an accident just after our tenth birthday. Ronnie Smith, who everybody said was the best trumpet player our school ever had. They buried his trumpet with him. And then there was Brother Ward. Every Wednesday night, when the pastor asked for testimonies, Brother Ward rose to his feet. Dressed in blue work pants and a flannel shirt, he gripped the pew in front of him and never said a word. He simply stood there, his broad shoulders shaking as tears rolled down his rough cheeks, and raised his hand toward heaven.

I don't often get back home these days. Whenever I do, I still visit that cemetery. My father

4 WEDNESDAY

For you are my lamp, O Lord; the Lord shall enlighten my darkness.
—2 Samuel 22:29-30 (NKJV)

5 THURSDAY

Likewise the Spirit helps us in our weakness. For we do not know what to pray for as we ought, but the Spirit himself intercedes for us with groanings too deep for words.
—Romans 8:26 (ESV)

6 FRIDAY

Whoever abides in me and I in him, he it is that bears much fruit. —John 15:5 (ESV)

7 SATURDAY

For everyone who asks receives; the one who seeks finds; and to the one who knocks, the door will be opened. —Luke 11:10 (NIV)

---

and grandmother are there now, too. But I've found that I don't have to be actually on that bench to heed the invitation to "come sit with us." I simply need to stop my bustle and find a quiet spot of my own. And remember.

—*Mary Lou Carney*

PRAYER REQUESTS _____

NOVEMBER

S	M	T	W	T	F	S
1	2	3	4	5	6	7
8	9	10	11	12	13	14
15	16	17	18	19	20	21
22	23	24	25	26	27	28
29	30					

OUR PRAYER
Lord, help me to rejoice in challenge and learn from adversity.

---

8 **SUNDAY** — "If you love those who love you, what credit is that to you?" —Luke 6:32 (NRSVCE)

---

9 **MONDAY** — I have fought the good fight, I have finished the race, I have kept the faith. —2 Timothy 4:7 (NIV)

---

10 **TUESDAY** — "Lord, you know all things; you know that I love you." Jesus said, "Feed my sheep." —John 21:17 (NIV)

TO WALK ON A BEACH IS, for me, a time of meditation. To stroll beside the waves is to listen to the voice of my soul.

Yesterday, I spent such a day at the beach. It was a time of evaluating my 43 years, my past with its victories and failures, its weaknesses and strengths. I was wondering about the future and my ability to cope with all the responsibilities that I could see ahead of me.

I was deep in thought when I saw a sight that amazed me. A balding man, middle-aged and athletic, was standing in the pounding surf. Facing the breakers, he braced as each wave hit him, a broad smile of joy on his face. But he had only one leg! Hopping back and forth as he battled each wave, he managed to keep his balance. His crutches lay behind him on the sand. Then a wave knocked him flat. As he struggled to stand, he laughed joyously, delighting in the battle.

The sight of this one-legged man in the surf spoke volumes to me. No matter how I might see myself injured by life—and we all are—no matter my weaknesses and failures, I have a choice. I

11
WEDNESDAY
VETERANS DAY

God makes his people strong. God gives his people peace. —Psalm 29:11 (MSG)

12
THURSDAY

Choose you this day whom ye will serve. —Joshua 24:15 (KJV)

13
FRIDAY

Then God surveyed everything He had made, savoring its beauty and appreciating its goodness. —Genesis 1:31 (VOICE)

14
SATURDAY

Fix your thoughts on what is true and good and right. —Philippians 4:8 (TLB)

---

can sit safely on the beach with my crutches, or I can boldly confront life's challenges.

Today, I have returned to my many responsibilities and tasks with joy, exulting in the demands of the day.

—*Scott Walker*

PRAYER REQUESTS _____

NOVEMBER

S	M	T	W	T	F	S
1	2	3	4	5	6	7
8	9	10	11	12	13	14
15	16	17	18	19	20	21
22	23	24	25	26	27	28
29	30					

GUIDEPOSTS DAILY PLANNER

OUR PRAYER
Dear Lord, make me more sensitive to the ways I can bring others comfort and healing from pain.

15 SUNDAY

Now then, stand still and see this great thing the Lord is about to do before your eyes! —1 Samuel 12:16 (NIV)

16 MONDAY

For there is nothing hidden that will not be disclosed, and nothing concealed that will not be known or brought out into the open. —Luke 8:17 (NIV)

17 TUESDAY

Be kind and compassionate to one another, forgiving each other, just as in Christ God forgave you. —Ephesians 4:32 (NIV)

ONE DAY, a former student approached me with a request for help. He took a small photo from his wallet and handed it to me. It was of his daughter and his only grandson, he told me; they had moved in with him after she divorced. Then with tears, he explained that, though they had been close, he didn't know what to do for his daughter.

As I looked from his face to the picture, I was seeing myself as a teenage boy lying face down on my parents' bed, weeping my heart out for a whole afternoon. I had just learned that my parents were getting a divorce. There was no one to help me with my pain.

Out of that memory came my answer. "What would you do for your daughter if, instead of this, your son-in-law had been killed in a car accident? The failure of a marriage is like a death in the family—but without the usual support system. People don't usually come with hugs and tears and food, or send cards, or even telephone when there's a divorce. But the pain is just as great."

"Thanks," he said as he put the picture back in

18 WEDNESDAY
When hard pressed, I cried to the LORD; he brought me into a spacious place.
—Psalm 118:5 (NIV)

19 THURSDAY
Whatever you do, work at it with all your heart, as working for the Lord, not for human masters, since you know that you will receive an inheritance from the Lord as a reward. It is the Lord Christ you are serving. —Colossians 3:23–24 (NIV)

20 FRIDAY
You need to persevere so that when you have done the will of God, you will receive what he has promised. —Hebrews 10:36 (NIV)

21 SATURDAY
If any of you lacks wisdom, let him ask of God, who gives to all liberally and without reproach, and it will be given to him. —James 1:5 (NKJV)

---

his wallet. "I think I know exactly what my daughter needs from me." As I watched him head for the parking lot, I was grateful that God had created out of my suffering a larger compassion for people affected by the pain of a failed marriage.

—*Kenneth Chafin*

PRAYER REQUESTS

NOVEMBER

S	M	T	W	T	F	S
1	2	3	4	5	6	7
8	9	10	11	12	13	14
15	16	17	18	19	20	21
22	23	24	25	26	27	28
29	30					

OUR PRAYER

You who fed the multitude, we come to Your table with thanks this day, one family strengthened and renewed by Your grace.

---

22 SUNDAY
NATIONAL BIBLE WEEK BEGINS

Command those who are rich in this present world not to be arrogant nor to put their hope in wealth. —1 Timothy 6:17 (NIV)

---

23 MONDAY
GUIDEPOSTS THANKSGIVING DAY OF PRAYER

Bear with me a little longer, and I will show you that there is more to be said in God's behalf. —Job 36:2 (NIV)

---

24 TUESDAY

He says to the snow, "Fall on the earth." —Job 37:6 (NIV)

THE CORNERSTONE OF OUR Thanksgiving feast in Hawaii was potato dressing. The recipe had entered our family via my *tai kung* or great-grandfather, an immigrant from Guangdong, China, who had learned it from the New England missionary family for whom he had cooked at the turn of the century.

The family recipe went with me when I moved to New York. For years, the dressing graced our Thanksgiving table, enjoyed by my husband, myself, and our growing family, which now included our small son, Tim, my brother, Jerry, and his wife, Donna.

When Jerry and Donna moved to Oregon (taking the recipe along), I grumbled to a girlfriend about the futility of making turkey and dressing for three. "Could I join you?" my friend asked, and kept coming for six Thanksgivings. By the time she moved to Wisconsin with my recipe and her two babies, I had gained an appreciation for the dressing's miraculous ability to change strangers into participants in an ongoing Thanksgiving tradition.

This year, new friends will join our family at the table. The Bertrands will bring Haitian rice and a cousin or three; the Gaspariks, a Southern-style pecan pie; Una will cook up Shanghai noodles; my

NOVEMBER 2026

25
WEDNESDAY

Be transformed by the renewing of your mind. —Romans 12:2 (NKJV)

26
THURSDAY
THANKSGIVING

For I am sure that neither death nor life, nor angels nor rulers, nor things present nor things to come, nor powers, nor height nor depth, nor anything else in all creation, will be able to separate us from the love of God in Christ Jesus our Lord. —Romans 8:38–39 (ESV)

27
FRIDAY

They shall praise His name with dancing; they shall sing praises to Him with tambourine and lyre. —Psalm 149:3 (NASB)

28
SATURDAY

So from now on we regard no one from a worldly point of view. —2 Corinthians 5:16 (NIV)

---

brother's son Brian, visiting from college, will bring his two hungry roommates. And at the center of the feast will be my *tai kung's* potato dressing, still feeding and binding our family across the years and the miles in marvelous ways.

—*Linda Ching Sledge*

PRAYER REQUESTS _____

NOVEMBER

S	M	T	W	T	F	S
1	2	3	4	5	6	7
8	9	10	11	12	13	14
15	16	17	18	19	20	21
22	23	24	25	26	27	28
29	30					

GUIDEPOSTS DAILY PLANNER

If it were not so, I would have told you. I go to prepare a place for you.
—JOHN 14:2 (NKJV)

A PRAYER FOR DECEMBER

Like the star
That guided
The wise men that night
Lord, send your light
To guide us
Through the dark
And home again.

UNKNOWN

LIVING A NEW LIFE
The Power of Acceptance

My husband, Norman Vincent Peale, and I had been married for 63 years on the Christmas Eve when he passed. I was aware that day that his life on this earth was coming to an end. His physical body had been wearing down, and the doctor was coming to our farm frequently.

Outside, the sky was growing dark with approaching night. Inside, various members of our family were quietly coming in and out of the bedroom where Norman lay. When Norman found it increasingly difficult to breathe, everyone left the room except me. As his struggle intensified, I leaned close to him. "It's all right," I whispered in his ear, "you can let go now."

His breathing grew slower. And slower. Slower. There was no sign, yet that was a sign. The breathing had stopped. I called the family.

"What do we do now?" my daughter Margaret asked.

"Pray," I said. "We pray." And I turned to the doctor and asked him to lead us, which he did, simply and beautifully, speaking to God with gratitude for the life of Norman Vincent Peale.

And that was it. Except it wasn't. A death? Yes, but the beginning of a new life for Norman. "Because I live," Jesus said, "ye shall live also" (John 14:19, KJV). I took hold of those words and held them fast. I hold them close now.

And so must you.

—Ruth Stafford Peale

DECEMBER 2026

SUNDAY	MONDAY	TUESDAY	WEDNESDAY	THURSDAY	FRIDAY	SATURDAY
		1	2	3	4 HANUKKAH BEGINS AT SUNDOWN	5
6 2ND SUNDAY IN ADVENT	7	8	9	10	11	12
13 3RD SUNDAY IN ADVENT	14	15	16	17	18	19
20 4TH SUNDAY IN ADVENT	21 WINTER BEGINS	22	23	24 CHRISTMAS EVE	25 CHRISTMAS	26
27	28	29	30	31 NEW YEAR'S EVE		

NOTES

NOVEMBER

S	M	T	W	T	F	S
1	2	3	4	5	6	7
8	9	10	11	12	13	14
15	16	17	18	19	20	21
22	23	24	25	26	27	28
29	30					

JANUARY 2027

S	M	T	W	T	F	S
					1	2
3	4	5	6	7	8	9
10	11	12	13	14	15	16
17	18	19	20	21	22	23
24/31	25	26	27	28	29	30

GUIDEPOSTS DAILY PLANNER

OUR PRAYER
Father, as we anticipate the coming of Your Son, fill every dark corner of our preparation with Your light.

---

29 SUNDAY
1ST SUNDAY IN ADVENT

When Jesus spoke again to the people, he said, "I am the light of the world. Whoever follows me will never walk in darkness but will have the light of life." —John 8:12 (NIV)

---

30 MONDAY

Taste and see that the Lord is good; blessed is the one who takes refuge in him. —Psalm 34:8 (NIV)

DECEMBER 1 TUESDAY

Behold, all things have become new. —2 Corinthians 5:17 (NKJV)

Early on this first Sunday in Advent, I sit alone in the dark living room. Thinking about the weeks ahead, I go to the hall closet and pull out the box that holds our family's most beloved Christmas treasure, a wooden structure 3 feet high called a Christmas carousel. My father purchased this beautiful, hand-carved creation in Germany many years ago.

As I place the carousel in its traditional spot on the dining room table, it occurs to me that I might allow myself a small Advent celebration before the house erupts into its Sunday morning busyness. I light the candles on the bottom tier, and soon the rising heat turns the wooden blades at the top of the carousel. As the blades spin, carved shepherds and wise men and angels on the three tiers begin to turn, as though traveling toward the Holy Family on the highest tier. In the soft candlelight, the journey to Christmas seems so simple, yet I know full well how exhausting the season can be. *What can I do, God, to find the real Christmas amid the frantic activity?* I pray. I wait in the stillness for an answer.

Focus on the light, God seems to say. Clear the path that leads to the real Christmas by saying no

2 WEDNESDAY

Never will I leave you; never will I forsake you. —Hebrews 13:5 (NIV)

3 THURSDAY

They who wait for the Lord shall renew their strength; they shall mount up with wings like eagles; they shall run and not be weary; they shall walk and not faint. —Isaiah 40:31 (ESV)

4 FRIDAY
HANUKKAH BEGINS AT SUNDOWN

Lord, save us! Lord, grant us success! —Psalm 118:25 (NIV)

5 SATURDAY

Remember me with favor, my God. —Nehemiah 13:31 (NIV)

---

to the events that hold little meaning. Bring the family together for the cookie-baking, tree-trimming, and visits to shut-ins you remember from your childhood. Above all, keep your eyes set on the light of the manger where the Christ Child waits.

—*Pam Kidd*

PRAYER REQUESTS _____

DECEMBER

S	M	T	W	T	F	S
		1	2	3	4	5
6	7	8	9	10	11	12
13	14	15	16	17	18	19
20	21	22	23	24	25	26
27	28	29	30	31		

GUIDEPOSTS DAILY PLANNER

OUR PRAYER

Lord, let us make memories that will forever fill our hearts with Christmas.

6
SUNDAY
2ND SUNDAY IN ADVENT

Mary treasured up all these things and pondered them in her heart. —Luke 2:19 (NIV)

7
MONDAY

Then God said, "Let the waters abound with an abundance of living creatures, and let birds fly above the earth across the face of the firmament of the heavens." —Genesis 1:20 (NKJV)

8
TUESDAY

For great is his love toward us, and the faithfulness of the Lord endures forever. Praise the Lord. —Psalm 117:2 (NIV)

By the second Sunday in Advent, decorating Kidd-style is in full swing. "Keep moving or Mom will decorate you," my husband, David, teases the kids, but I'm too consumed with seeking perfection to laugh.

Dashing through the dining room with my arms full of garland, I pause to find my daughter, Keri, sitting there. "Mama," she asks, "do you remember this old Snoopy ornament?"

How could I forget? It was the year Keri was four. A month before the holidays, we had gone to an amusement park with another family. Their little son, Ty, had his heart set on a toy Snoopy dog from the ball-toss booth, but no one in our group could hit the mark. Ty went home tearful. Later, during Keri's visit to Santa at the mall, she asked for only one thing—a Snoopy for Ty. Santa not only brought Ty a Snoopy, but that ornament for Keri to commend her for her Christmas spirit.

I look at my daughter, now in college, sitting in my Christmas clutter. "Keri, why don't you light the carousel? It would be nice to sit down and rest for a minute." I know that as the tiny figures continue their pilgrimage toward the

9
WEDNESDAY

I praise you because I am fearfully and wonderfully made. —Psalm 139:14 (NIV)

10
THURSDAY

The Son radiates God's own glory and expresses the very character of God, and he sustains everything by the mighty power of his command. —Hebrews 1:3 (NLT)

11
FRIDAY

For whosoever shall call upon the name of the Lord shall be saved. —Romans 10:13 (KJV)

12
SATURDAY

Thanks be to God for his inexpressible gift! —2 Corinthians 9:15 (ESV)

Christ, I can reroute my own journey.

On this second Sunday in Advent, I have a choice. I can run myself ragged trying to create a picture-perfect Christmas, or I can relax and bask in the glow of love and family—memories in the making.

—*Pam Kidd*

PRAYER REQUESTS

DECEMBER

S	M	T	W	T	F	S
		1	2	3	4	5
6	7	8	9	10	11	12
13	14	15	16	17	18	19
20	21	22	23	24	25	26
27	28	29	30	31		

OUR PRAYER
Father, let my gifts to others reflect Your timeless love.

---

13 SUNDAY — *3RD SUNDAY IN ADVENT*

So then, brothers and sisters, stand firm and hold fast to the teachings we passed on to you, whether by word of mouth or by letter. —2 Thessalonians 2:15 (NIV)

---

14 MONDAY

I wait quietly before God, for my victory comes from him. —Psalm 62:1 (NLT)

---

15 TUESDAY

I will repay you for the years the locusts have eaten—the great locust and the young locust, the other locusts and the locust swarm—my great army that I sent among you. —Joel 2:25 (NIV)

ON THIS THIRD SUNDAY in Advent, I'm feeling good about my Christmas journey. Now it's time to concentrate on shopping. Reviewing last year's list, panic sets in. Too many presents, too little time, even less money! Buying gifts for some of the people on my list seems like an exercise in futility.

Take my Aunt Ann. Retired, living in an apartment, she has everything she needs and not an inch of room for anything extra. David's Aunt Kate is in a similar situation. There's nothing we can give her that she can't buy for herself.

I know from experience that the all-around stress of gift-giving can create a roadblock between me and the light of the Christ Child. *Father,* I ask, *show me Your way to give.*

I make myself a cup of spice tea and go into the living room to regroup. I think of Aunt Ann filling her car with day-old baked goods and making deliveries to the poor in her south Georgia town. Aunt Kate is in her eighties now, but in other days what feasts she set before us!

Suddenly, a new kind of giving is ignited in my heart. I will provide Christmas for a needy child in

16
WEDNESDAY

Surely I am with you always, to the very end of the age. —Matthew 28:20 (NIV)

17
THURSDAY

Do not remember the former things, nor consider the things of old. Behold, I will do a new thing, now it shall spring forth; shall you not know it? I will even make a road in the wilderness and rivers in the desert. —Isaiah 43:18–19 (NKJV)

18
FRIDAY

If any household is too small for a whole lamb, they must share one with their nearest neighbor. —Exodus 12:4 (NIV)

19
SATURDAY

An intelligent heart acquires knowledge, and the ear of the wise seeks knowledge. —Proverbs 18:15 (ESV)

---

honor of Aunt Ann and present her with a detailed description. Aunt Kate still entertains frequently; she would love a basket of homemade goodies to share with her friends.

To be a part of this thing called Christmas, I will choose symbols of the life-gifts the people on my list have given to me and my family.

—*Pam Kidd*

PRAYER REQUESTS _____

DECEMBER

S	M	T	W	T	F	S
		1	2	3	4	5
6	7	8	9	10	11	12
13	14	15	16	17	18	19
20	21	22	23	24	25	26
27	28	29	30	31		

OUR PRAYER

Father, give me opportunity to see how love looks when we put others first.

---

20 **SUNDAY** — 4TH SUNDAY IN ADVENT

Taking the child in his arms, [Jesus] said to them, "Whoever welcomes one of these little children in my name welcomes me." —Mark 9:36–37 (NIV)

---

21 **MONDAY** — WINTER BEGINS

It is good for the heart to be strengthened by grace. —Hebrews 13:9 (ESV)

---

22 **TUESDAY**

Meanwhile we groan, longing to be clothed instead with our heavenly dwelling. —2 Corinthians 5:2 (NIV)

On this fourth Sunday of Advent, the house is decorated, the presents wrapped. As my son, Brock, says, "It's time to kick back and enjoy Christmas."

But earlier today, instead of "kicking back," I willingly entered the mayhem of commercial Christmas. After church, I went to the most hectic of all holiday places, the mall. Everywhere there were lights and glitter, elves, and big, colored balls. The music was loud. At Santa's village, kids stood in a long line.

"May I help you?" a young man asked when I reached a department store. I explained my need for a tie, and the clerk made suggestions until one was chosen. "Have a great Christmas!" he said. Later, in the gift-wrap line, the spirit was the same. Smiles, and laughter, and "Happy holidays!"

Every year, I purposely save a bit of my shopping until right before Christmas because I love the rush, the feel, the way people who usually don't even look to the right or to the left look straight at me and smile. The spirit of Christmas shows us what our world would look like if we followed

23
WEDNESDAY

In your presence there is fullness of joy; in your right hand are pleasures forevermore. —Psalm 16:11 (NRSVUE)

24
THURSDAY
CHRISTMAS EVE

Let us run with perseverance the race marked out for us, fixing our eyes on Jesus, the pioneer and perfecter of faith. —Hebrews 12:1–2 (NIV)

25
FRIDAY
CHRISTMAS

Praise be to the God and Father of our Lord Jesus Christ, who has blessed us in the heavenly realms with every spiritual blessing in Christ. —Ephesians 1:3 (NIV)

26
SATURDAY

Each of you should use whatever gift you have received to serve others, as faithful stewards of God's grace in its various forms. —1 Peter 4:10 (NIV)

Jesus's lead every day to love, love, love.

So before this Christmas passes, go to the mall or to some gathering place. Take a bag of smiles and give them to everyone you meet. The spirit of Christmas is waiting for you.

—*Pam Kidd*

PRAYER REQUESTS _____

DECEMBER

S	M	T	W	T	F	S
		1	2	3	4	5
6	7	8	9	10	11	12
13	14	15	16	17	18	19
20	21	22	23	24	25	26
27	28	29	30	31		

OUR PRAYER

*God of changes who never changes, hold my heart
in Your hands so that I shall not fear.*

---

27 SUNDAY

Even the Son of Man did not come to be served, but to serve, and to give his life as a ransom for many. —Mark 10:45 (NIV)

---

28 MONDAY

When I look at the night sky and see the work of your fingers—the moon and the stars you set in place—what are mere mortals that you should think about them, human beings that you should care for them? —Psalm 8:3–4 (NLT)

---

29 TUESDAY

Sometimes there is a phenomenon of which they say, "Look, this one is new!" —Ecclesiastes 1:10 (JPS)

NEVER HAS THERE BEEN a time in my life with so many changes. For one thing, the greenhouse where I used to grow orchids has come down to make room for a new garage. I hadn't exactly planned it, but the orchids died in one of the hard freezes we had last winter. And then the friend who introduced me to orchids died himself. So these days I earn my green equity outdoors.

Then there's Babu. This half-pint pup came into my life because my beloved Ashley passed on in January. Two months of Yorkie-free life was about all I could handle, so I'm back training a puppy. Babu tries to help me in the garden but gets into every stickle burr on the acre. He doesn't yet know how to care for his Yorkie coiffure.

The biggest change of all has been in my career. I went to half-time at Yale to have more time to share the things that God has been doing in my life. And more time to love a puppy. And more time to transform a weedy patch into a wildflower garden.

30
WEDNESDAY

But godliness with contentment is great gain. —1 Timothy 6:6 (ESV)

31
THURSDAY

NEW YEAR'S EVE

The LORD . . . lifteth up. —1 Samuel 2:7 (KJV)

JAN 2027

1
FRIDAY

NEW YEAR'S DAY

A desire accomplished is sweet to the soul. —Proverbs 13:19 (NKJV)

2
SATURDAY

Teach them to your children, talking about them when you sit at home and when you walk along the road. . . . —Deuteronomy 11:19 (NIV)

The oddest thing of all—for a year with so many changes—is that although I've grieved, I've not been afraid. It's as if each step were ordered and planned and linked to the next. I wonder what changes next year will bring?

—*Diane Komp*

PRAYER REQUESTS _____

_____

_____

DECEMBER

S	M	T	W	T	F	S
		1	2	3	4	5
6	7	8	9	10	11	12
13	14	15	16	17	18	19
20	21	22	23	24	25	26
27	28	29	30	31		

GUIDEPOSTS DAILY PLANNER

JANUARY 2027

SUNDAY	MONDAY	TUESDAY	WEDNESDAY	THURSDAY	FRIDAY	SATURDAY
					1 NEW YEAR'S DAY	2
3	4	5	6 EPIPHANY	7	8	9
10	11	12	13	14	15	16
17	18 MARTIN LUTHER KING JR. DAY	19	20	21	22	23
24 / 31	25	26	27	28	29	30

FEBRUARY 2027

SUNDAY	MONDAY	TUESDAY	WEDNESDAY	THURSDAY	FRIDAY	SATURDAY
	1	2	3	4	5	6
7	8	9	10 ASH WEDNESDAY	11	12 ABRAHAM LINCOLN'S BIRTHDAY	13
14 VALENTINE'S DAY	15 PRESIDENTS' DAY	16	17	18	19	20
21	22 GEORGE WASHINGTON'S BIRTHDAY	23	24	25	26	27
28						

MARCH 2027

SUNDAY	MONDAY	TUESDAY	WEDNESDAY	THURSDAY	FRIDAY	SATURDAY
	1	2	3	4	5	6
7	8	9	10	11	12	13
14 DAYLIGHT SAVING TIME BEGINS	15	16	17 ST. PATRICK'S DAY	18	19	20 SPRING BEGINS
21 PALM SUNDAY	22	23	24	25 MAUNDY THURSDAY	26 GOOD FRIDAY	27
28 EASTER	29	30	31			

APRIL 2027

SUNDAY	MONDAY	TUESDAY	WEDNESDAY	THURSDAY	FRIDAY	SATURDAY
				1	2	3
4	5	6	7	8	9	10
11	12	13	14	15	16	17
18	19	20	21 PASSOVER BEGINS AT SUNDOWN	22 EARTH DAY	23	24
25	26	27	28	29	30	

2027 CALENDAR

JANUARY
S	M	T	W	T	F	S
					1	2
3	4	5	6	7	8	9
10	11	12	13	14	15	16
17	18	19	20	21	22	23
24/31	25	26	27	28	29	30

FEBRUARY
S	M	T	W	T	F	S
	1	2	3	4	5	6
7	8	9	10	11	12	13
14	15	16	17	18	19	20
21	22	23	24	25	26	27
28						

MARCH
S	M	T	W	T	F	S
	1	2	3	4	5	6
7	8	9	10	11	12	13
14	15	16	17	18	19	20
21	22	23	24	25	26	27
28	29	30	31			

APRIL
S	M	T	W	T	F	S
				1	2	3
4	5	6	7	8	9	10
11	12	13	14	15	16	17
18	19	20	21	22	23	24
25	26	27	28	29	30	

MAY
S	M	T	W	T	F	S
						1
2	3	4	5	6	7	8
9	10	11	12	13	14	15
16	17	18	19	20	21	22
23/30	24/31	25	26	27	28	29

JUNE
S	M	T	W	T	F	S
		1	2	3	4	5
6	7	8	9	10	11	12
13	14	15	16	17	18	19
20	21	22	23	24	25	26
27	28	29	30			

JULY
S	M	T	W	T	F	S
				1	2	3
4	5	6	7	8	9	10
11	12	13	14	15	16	17
18	19	20	21	22	23	24
25	26	27	28	29	30	31

AUGUST
S	M	T	W	T	F	S
1	2	3	4	5	6	7
8	9	10	11	12	13	14
15	16	17	18	19	20	21
22	23	24	25	26	27	28
29	30	31				

SEPTEMBER
S	M	T	W	T	F	S
			1	2	3	4
5	6	7	8	9	10	11
12	13	14	15	16	17	18
19	20	21	22	23	24	25
26	27	28	29	30		

OCTOBER
S	M	T	W	T	F	S
					1	2
3	4	5	6	7	8	9
10	11	12	13	14	15	16
17	18	19	20	21	22	23
24/31	25	26	27	28	29	30

NOVEMBER
S	M	T	W	T	F	S
	1	2	3	4	5	6
7	8	9	10	11	12	13
14	15	16	17	18	19	20
21	22	23	24	25	26	27
28	29	30				

DECEMBER
S	M	T	W	T	F	S
			1	2	3	4
5	6	7	8	9	10	11
12	13	14	15	16	17	18
19	20	21	22	23	24	25
26	27	28	29	30	31	

2028 CALENDAR

JANUARY
S	M	T	W	T	F	S
						1
2	3	4	5	6	7	8
9	10	11	12	13	14	15
16	17	18	19	20	21	22
23/30	24/31	25	26	27	28	29

FEBRUARY
S	M	T	W	T	F	S
		1	2	3	4	5
6	7	8	9	10	11	12
13	14	15	16	17	18	19
20	21	22	23	24	25	26
27	28	29				

MARCH
S	M	T	W	T	F	S
			1	2	3	4
5	6	7	8	9	10	11
12	13	14	15	16	17	18
19	20	21	22	23	24	25
26	27	28	29	30	31	

APRIL
S	M	T	W	T	F	S
						1
2	3	4	5	6	7	8
9	10	11	12	13	14	15
16	17	18	19	20	21	22
23/30	24	25	26	27	28	29

MAY
S	M	T	W	T	F	S
	1	2	3	4	5	6
7	8	9	10	11	12	13
14	15	16	17	18	19	20
21	22	23	24	25	26	27
28	29	30	31			

JUNE
S	M	T	W	T	F	S
				1	2	3
4	5	6	7	8	9	10
11	12	13	14	15	16	17
18	19	20	21	22	23	24
25	26	27	28	29	30	

JULY
S	M	T	W	T	F	S
						1
2	3	4	5	6	7	8
9	10	11	12	13	14	15
16	17	18	19	20	21	22
23/30	24/31	25	26	27	28	29

AUGUST
S	M	T	W	T	F	S
		1	2	3	4	5
6	7	8	9	10	11	12
13	14	15	16	17	18	19
20	21	22	23	24	25	26
27	28	29	30	31		

SEPTEMBER
S	M	T	W	T	F	S
					1	2
3	4	5	6	7	8	9
10	11	12	13	14	15	16
17	18	19	20	21	22	23
24	25	26	27	28	29	30

OCTOBER
S	M	T	W	T	F	S
1	2	3	4	5	6	7
8	9	10	11	12	13	14
15	16	17	18	19	20	21
22	23	24	25	26	27	28
29	30	31				

NOVEMBER
S	M	T	W	T	F	S
			1	2	3	4
5	6	7	8	9	10	11
12	13	14	15	16	17	18
19	20	21	22	23	24	25
26	27	28	29	30		

DECEMBER
S	M	T	W	T	F	S
					1	2
3	4	5	6	7	8	9
10	11	12	13	14	15	16
17	18	19	20	21	22	23
24/31	25	26	27	28	29	30

HOLIDAYS & IMPORTANT DATES

HOLIDAY	2027	2028	2029
New Year's Day	Friday, January 1	Saturday, January 1	Monday, January 1
Epiphany	Wednesday, January 6	Thursday, January 6	Saturday, January 6
Martin Luther King Jr. Day	Monday, January 18	Monday, January 17	Monday, January 15
Ash Wednesday	Wednesday, February 10	Wednesday, March 1	Wednesday, February 14
Abraham Lincoln's Birthday	Friday, February 12	Saturday, February 12	Monday, February 12
Valentine's Day	Sunday, February 14	Monday, February 14	Wednesday, February 14
Presidents' Day	Monday, February 15	Monday, February 21	Monday, February 19
George Washington's Birthday	Monday, February 22	Tuesday, February 22	Thursday, February 22
Daylight Saving Time Begins	Sunday, March 14	Sunday, March 12	Sunday, March 11
St. Patrick's Day	Wednesday, March 17	Friday, March 17	Saturday, March 17
Spring Begins	Saturday, March 20	Sunday, March 19	Tuesday, March 20
Palm Sunday	Sunday, March 21	Sunday, April 9	Sunday, March 25
Maundy Thursday	Thursday, March 25	Thursday, April 13	Thursday, March 29
Good Friday	Friday, March 26	Friday, April 14	Friday, March 30
Easter	Sunday, March 28	Sunday, April 16	Sunday, April 1
Passover Begins at Sundown	Wednesday, April 21	Monday , April 10	Friday March 30
Earth Day	Thursday, April 22	Saturday, April 22	Sunday, April 22
National Day of Prayer	Thursday, May 6	Thursday, May 4	Thursday, May 3
Mother's Day	Sunday, May 9	Sunday, May 14	Sunday, May 13
Ascension Day	Thursday, May 6	Thursday, May 25	Thursday, May 10
Pentecost	Sunday, May 16	Sunday, June 4	Sunday, May 20
Memorial Day	Monday, May 31	Monday, May 29	Monday, May 28
Flag Day	Monday, June 14	Wednesday, June 14	Thursday June 14
Juneteenth	Saturday, June 19	Monday, June 19	Tuesday, June 19
Father's Day	Sunday, June 20	Sunday, June 18	Sunday, June 17
Summer Begins	Monday, June 21	Tuesday, June 20	Wednesday, June 20
Independence Day	Sunday, July 4	Tuesday, July 4	Wednesday, July 4

HOLIDAYS & IMPORTANT DATES

HOLIDAY	2027	2028	2029
Labor Day	Monday, September 6	Monday, September 4	Monday, September 3
Rosh Hashanah Begins at Sundown	Friday, October 1	Wednesday, September 20	Sunday, September 9
Citizenship Day	Friday, September 17	Sunday, September 17	Monday, September 17
Fall Begins	Thursday, September 23	Friday, September 22	Saturday, September 22
World Communion Sunday	Sunday, October 3	Sunday, October 1	Sunday, October 7
Yom Kippur Begins at Sundown	Sunday, October 10	Friday, September 29	Tuesday, September 18
United Nations Day	Sunday, October 24	Tuesday, October 24	Wednesday, October 24
Halloween	Sunday, October 31	Tuesday, October 31	Wednesday, October 31
All Saints' Day	Monday, November 1	Wednesday, November 1	Thursday, November 1
Daylight Saving Time Ends	Sunday, November 7	Sunday, November 5	Sunday, November 4
All Souls' Day	Tuesday, November 2	Thursday, November 2	Friday, November 2
Election Day	Tuesday, November 2	Tuesday, November 7	Tuesday, November 6
Veterans Day	Thursday, November 11	Saturday, November 11	Monday, November 12
National Bible Week Begins	Sunday, November 21	Sunday, November 19	Sunday, November 18
Guideposts Thanksgiving Day of Prayer	Monday, November 22	Monday, November 20	Monday, November 19
Thanksgiving	Thursday, November 25	Thursday, November 23	Thursday, November 22
1st Sunday in Advent	Sunday, November 28	Sunday, December 3	Sunday, December 2
2nd Sunday in Advent	Sunday, December 5	Sunday, December 10	Sunday, December 9
3rd Sunday in Advent	Sunday, December 12	Sunday, December 17	Sunday, December 16
4th Sunday in Advent	Sunday, December 19	Sunday, December 24	Sunday, December 23
Winter Begins	Tuesday, December 21	Thursday, December 21	Friday, December 21
Hanukkah Begins at Sundown	Friday, December 24	Tuesday, December 12	Saturday, December 1
Christmas Eve	Friday, December 24	Sunday, December 24	Monday, December 24
Christmas	Saturday, December 25	Monday, December 25	Tuesday, December 25
New Year's Eve	Friday, December 31	Sunday, December 31	Monday, December 31

BIRTHDAYS

JANUARY
_____
_____
_____
_____
_____

FEBRUARY
_____
_____
_____
_____
_____

MARCH
_____
_____
_____
_____
_____

APRIL
_____
_____
_____
_____
_____

MAY
_____
_____
_____
_____
_____

JUNE
_____
_____
_____
_____
_____

JULY
_____
_____
_____
_____
_____

AUGUST
_____
_____
_____
_____
_____

SEPTEMBER
_____
_____
_____
_____
_____

OCTOBER
_____
_____
_____
_____
_____

NOVEMBER
_____
_____
_____
_____
_____

DECEMBER
_____
_____
_____
_____
_____

FAMILY & FRIENDS

NAME ADDRESS TELEPHONE

FAMILY & FRIENDS

NAME ADDRESS TELEPHONE

PRAYER REQUESTS

Guideposts Daily Planner 2026

Published by Guideposts
100 Reserve Road, Suite E200, Danbury, CT 06810
Guideposts.org

Copyright © 2026 by Guideposts. All rights reserved.

This book, or parts thereof, may not be reproduced, stored in a retrieval system, or transmitted in any form or by any means, electronic, mechanical, photocopying, recording, or otherwise, without the written permission of the publisher.

Acknowledgments

Every attempt has been made to credit the sources of copyrighted material used in this book. If any such acknowledgment has been inadvertently omitted or miscredited, receipt of such information would be appreciated.

Scripture quotations marked (CEV) are taken from *Holy Bible: Contemporary English Version*. Copyright © 1995 American Bible Society.

Scripture quotations marked (CSB) are taken from *The Christian Standard Bible*, copyright © 2017 by Holman Bible Publishers. Used by permission.

Scripture quotations marked (ESV) are taken from the *Holy Bible, English Standard Version*. Copyright © 2001 by Crossway Bibles, a division of Good News Publishers. Used by permission. All rights reserved.

Scripture quotations marked (GNT) are taken from the *Good News Translation*® (Today's English Version, Second Edition) © 1992 American Bible Society.

Scripture quotations marked (JPS) are taken from *Tanakh: A New Translation of the Holy Scriptures according to the Traditional Hebrew Text*. Copyright © 1985 by the Jewish Publication Society. All rights reserved.

Scripture quotations marked (KJV) are taken from the *King James Version of the Bible*.

Scripture quotations marked (MSG) are taken from T*he Message*. Copyright © 1993, 2002, 2018 by Eugene H. Peterson.

Scripture quotations marked (NABRE) are taken from the *New American Bible*, revised edition, © 2010, 1991, 1986, 1970 Confraternity of Christian Doctrine, Inc., Washington, DC. All rights reserved.

Scripture quotations marked (NASB) are taken from the *New American Standard Bible*®, Copyright © 1960, 1971, 1977, 1995, 2020 by The Lockman Foundation. All rights reserved.

Scripture quotations marked (NIV) are taken from *The Holy Bible, New International Version*®*, NIV*®. Copyright © 1973, 1978, 1984, 2011 by Biblica, Inc. Used by permission. All rights reserved worldwide.

Scripture quotations marked (NKJV) are taken from *The Holy Bible, New King James Version*. Copyright © 1982 by Thomas Nelson. Used by permission. All rights reserved.

Scripture quotations marked (NLT) are taken from *Holy Bible, New Living Translation*. Copyright © 1996, 2004, 2007, 2015 by Tyndale House Foundation. Used by permission of Tyndale House Publishers Inc., Carol Stream, Illinois. All rights reserved.

Scripture quotations marked (NRSVCE) are taken from the *New Revised Standard Version Bible: Catholic Edition*, copyright © 1989, 1993 the Division of Christian Education of the National Council of the Churches of Christ in the United States of America. Used by permission. All rights reserved.

Scripture quotations marked (NRSVUE) are taken from the *New Revised Standard Version, Updated Edition*. Copyright © 2021 by National Council of Churches of Christ in the United States of America. Used by permission. All rights reserved worldwide.

Scripture quotations marked (RSV) are taken from the *Revised Standard Version of the Bible*. Copyright © 1946, 1952, 1971 by the Division of Christian Education of the National Council of the Churches of Christ in the United States of America. Used by permission.

Scripture quotations marked (TLB) are taken from *The Living Bible*. Copyright © 1971 by Tyndale House Publishers, Inc., Carol Stream, Illinois. All rights reserved.

Scripture quotations marked (VOICE) are taken from *The Voice Bible*, copyright © 2012 Thomas Nelson, Inc. The Voice™ translation copyright © 2012 Ecclesia Bible Society. All rights reserved.

Scripture quotations marked (WE) are taken from the *Worldwide English (New Testament)*, © 1969, 1971, 1996, 1998 by SOON Educational Publications.

Cover and interior design by Müllerhaus; cover photo by Noppawat Tom Charoensinphon, Getty Images. Monthly page opener photos: January, Fabrice Villard/Unsplash; February, Unsplash; March, coldsnowstorm/Getty Images; April, Anna Perfilova/Getty Images; May, Oksana Schmidt/Getty Images; June, ooyoo/Getty Images; July, gjohnstonphoto/Getty Images; August, Allec Gomez/Unsplash; September, borchee/Getty Images; October, Wirestock/Getty Images; November, Andrei Metelev/Getty Images; December, Marcel/Adobe Stock.

ISBN-13 - 978-1-961441-33-0

Printed and bound in China

A NOTE FROM THE EDITORS

We hope you enjoyed the *Guideposts Daily Planner*, published by Guideposts. For over 75 years, Guideposts, a nonprofit organization, has been driven by a vision of a world filled with hope. We aspire to be the voice of a trusted friend, a friend who makes you feel more hopeful and connected.

By making a purchase from Guideposts, you join our community in touching millions of lives, inspiring them to believe that all things are possible through faith, hope, and prayer. Your continued support allows us to provide uplifting resources to those in need. Whether through our communities, websites, apps, or publications, we inspire our audiences, bring them together, and comfort, uplift, entertain, and guide them. Visit us at guideposts.org to learn more.

We would love to hear from you. Write us at Guideposts, P.O. Box 5815, Harlan, Iowa 51593 or call us at (800) 932-2145. Did you love the *Guideposts Daily Planner*? Leave a review for this product on guideposts.org/shop. Your feedback helps others in our community find relevant products.

Find inspiration, find faith, find Guideposts.

Shop our best sellers and favorites at
guideposts.org/shop

or scan the QR code to go directly to our Shop